Colonial Hegemony and Indigenous Resistance in Chotanagpur (1858-1947)

Tribal Movements, Nationalist Upsurge, Evangelical Forces and their Enduring Legacies

Dr. Saurabh Mishra,
Smt. Pinki Devi,
Sh. Gurdev Singh,
Sh. Nitin Kumar

Made with ♥ on the Notion Press Platform

www.notionpress.com

CONTENTS

ABOUT THE AUTHOR

Dr. Saurabh Mishra is currently an Assistant Professor of History at Government College Salooni, District Chamba, H.P. He has been awarded doctorate degree for his thesis "Nature of Tribal Movements in Chotanagpur (1858-1947)" by the University of Lucknow in 2023. He has published 6 research papers in UGC CARE listed journals and presented much more in the national and international seminars and conferences. He has tremendous knowledge of Modern Indian history. This is his first academic book on tribal history.

Smt. Pinki Devi currently working as an Assistant Professor of Hindi at Government College Salooni, District Chamba, H.P. She is a renowned researcher and have published many articles and research papers on tribal and folk culture in several prestigious journals and conferences. She is working as an Assistant Professor since 2017.

Sh. Nitin Kumar is currently serving as a Post Graduate Teacher of History in Madhubani District of Bihar. He has qualified NET, CTET, BSTET, MPTET and BPSC TRE exams. He has immense knowledge of tribal movements and history of freedom struggle of India.

Sh. Gurdev Singh has served in the Indian Airforce for 20 years and is currently serving as an Assistant Professor of Political Science in Government Degree College Salooni, H.P. since 2023. His knowledge about tribal demands on political autonomy is immense and praiseworthy.

INTRODUCTION

The Chota Nagpur region is a plateau in eastern India, covering much of the recently created Jharkhand state, as well as the bordering areas of Orissa, West Bengal, Bihar and Chhattisgarh. Geo-historically, it was a part of Deccan plate, which broke free from the southern continent during the Cretaceous period. The region lies between 22^0 N to 25^0 30'N latitude and 83^047'E to 87^057'E longitude. The tropic of cancer passes through Ranchi (near Ormanjhi), capital of Jharkhand.

The Chota Nagpur plateau is one of the oldest landmasses on the earth. It is composed of Precambrian rocks that are more than 540 million years old. The plateau in its entirety lies between the basins of the Ganga and the Son Rivers to the north, and the Mahanadi River to the south. To the north of Chota Nagpur lie the Rajmahal hills; to the west lie the highlands of Chhattisgarh and plains of Uttar Pradesh; the river Damodar in the East borders the Chota Nagpur plateau and the hills of Kharsawan in the South.

The formation of the state of Jharkhand on 15 November 2000 (the birth anniversary of Birsa Munda and now celebrated as (National Tribal Day) is one of the most important events in the history of Chota Nagpur. Unlike other states, Jharkhand was neither created on a linguistic basis nor for administrative convenience. The creation of a new state was the result of a continuous struggle of the indigenous people of Chota Nagpur during the nineteenth and twentieth century for the protection of their rights over land and forests.

The state of Jharkhand is spread over a total area of 79714 square kilo-meters (7.79 million hectares), which constitutes 2.4 percent of the total geographical area of the country. As per the 2011 census, about 2.72 percent of the population of the country lives in this state. Jharkhand is divided into five administrative divisions, 24 districts, 36 sub-divisions, 260 blocks, 4423 panchayats, 32615 villages, 228 towns, 3 corporations and 37 Nagar Parishads/ Nagar Panchayats. The divisions include: South Chotanagpur (comprising 5 districts, including the state capital Ranchi), Singhbhum (3 districts), North Chotanagpur (7 districts), Palamau (3 districts), and Santhal Pargana (6 districts).

Initially, North Chotanagpur Division consisted of Hazaribagh district and South Chotanagpur Division consisted of Palamau, Ranchi, Lohardaga, Singhbhum districts and Santhal Parganas had Deoghar, Dumka and Sahebganj districts. After the creation of Jharkhand state, old districts have been split up for administrative convenience. Now, Hazaribagh district consists of seven districts namely Chatra, Koderma in the north; Giridih in the east; Bokaro and Dhanbad in the west; Ramgarh in the south and remaining portion in Hazaribagh district. Similarly, Ranchi district has been split up in Gumla and Lohardaga on the west, Khunti and Simdega in the south and rest is Ranchi district. Palamau division now consists of Latehar, Garhwa and Palamau districts, while Santhal Parganas have Deoghar, Dumka, Godda, Jamtara, Pakur and Sahebganj districts. Singhbhum has been divided into Seraikela, West Singhbhum and East Singhbhum districts.

The state is richly endowed with natural resources especially forests and mineral resources. It has one of the richest deposits of coal and iron ore in the country. Other mineral resources like graphite, magnetite, gold, silver, bauxite, uranium, mica, fireclay and copper are also found in the state. The state accounts for almost 40 percent of the nation's mineral reserves. Forest account for about 28 percent of its geographical area. It is also blessed with rich flora and fauna. The annual rainfall in the plateau is 1400 mm on an average. There are number of perennial rivers and streams flowing through the state. The important rivers are Damodar, Subarnarekha, Koel, Barakar, Sankh, Karo, Ajay & Mayurakshi.

Figure 1. Location and extent of the Chotanagpur Plateau (dark solid line in Jharkhand, and dotted line in Orissa and West Bengal).

The Chota Nagpur region is the abode of various tribal groups. According to census 2011, Tribal population of Jharkhand is 86,45,042 which constitute 26.21 per cent of total population of Jharkhand. There are 32 tribes in Jharkhand: Asur, Baiga, Banjara, Bathudi, Bedia, Bhumij, Binjhia, Birhor, Birjiali, Chero, Chick-Baraik, Gond, Gorait, Ho, Kanwar, Karmali, Kharia, Kharwar, Khond, Kisan, Kol, Kora, Korwa, Lohar, Mahli, Mal-Paharia, Munda, Oraon, Parhaiya, Santhal, Sauria-Paharia and Savar.

L. P. Vidyarthi (1968) classified them on the basis of their association with specific cultural activities. It included hunter-gatherers (such as Birhor, Korwa, Kharia); shifting agriculturists (such as Sauria- Paharia); simple artisans (such as Mahli, Lohra, Karmali, Chick-Baraik); and settled agriculturists (such as Santhal, Munda, Oraons, Ho, Bhumij).

Table 1: Tribal Population of Jharkhand (As per census of India 2001)

S.no.	Tribes	population	percentage	Literacy
1.	Asur	10347	0.15	0.10
2.	Baiga	2508	0.03	0.01
3.	Banjara	374	0.005	0.003
4.	Bathudi	1114	0.016	0.01
5.	Bedia	83771	1.18	1.10
6.	Binjhia	12428	0.18	0.17
7.	Birhor	7514	0.11	0.04
8.	Bhumij	181329	2.56	2.65
9.	Birjiali	5365	0.08	0.05
10.	Chero	75540	1.07	1.00
11.	Chick-Baraik	44427	0.63	0.76
12.	Gond	52614	0.74	0.81
13.	Gorait	3957	0.06	0.06
14.	Ho	744850	10.5	9.92
15.	Karmali	56865	0.80	0.87
16.	Kharia	164022	2.31	2.96
17.	Kharwar	192024	2.71	1.87
18.	Khond	196	0.003	0.004
19.	Kisan	31568	0.45	0.31
20.	Kora	23192	0.33	0.28
21.	Korwa	27177	0.38	0.13
22.	Lohar	185008	2.61	2.47
23.	Mahli	121174	1.71	1.53
24.	Mal-Paharia	115093	1.62	0.80
25.	Munda	1049767	14.81	17.60
26.	Oraon	1390459	19.62	25.41
27.	Parhaiya	20786	0.29	0.09
28.	Santhal	2410509	34.01	28.15
29.	Sauria-Paharia	31050	0.44	0.22

S.no.	Tribes	population	percentage	Literacy
30.	Savar	6004	0.08	0.04
31.	Unclassified	36040	0.50	
	Total Tribal Population	70,87,072		

[**Note:** As per Scheduled Castes and Scheduled Tribes order (Amendment) Act 2002, Kanwar and Kol Tribes have been included in the list of Scheduled Tribes of Jharkhand in January 2003.]

THE IMPACT OF THE BRITISH POLICIES ON THE TRIBALS:

The British policies disturbed the traditional tribal system. The Tribal land system was marked by its community ownership of land and absence of the landlords. Although during the Mughal rule the formal allegiance of local rulers like the Nagvanshis and the Cheros was obtained but it never penetrated deep into the villages so as to exercise direct control. Different tribal communities were governing their own villages. This village based administrative system was usually governed by the village headman known as Munda and the priest known as Pahan. Network of 8-10 villages were headed by a Manki who used to solve disputes arising among different Mundas.

The pieces of land were held jointly by the villagers and there was no concept of an individual holding of land. Different portions of land were earmarked for different purposes, like some portion of land was marked as 'rajhas', the produce of which was reserved to be sent to the king as tribute; certain portion was reserved for religious activities called 'sarana land'; and some portion of land for community dancing and celebration known as 'akharas land'.

Besides, the tribes of Chota Nagpur had their Parha panchayats under Manki or Munda. Parha had access to all important welfare activities such as security, hunting, fairs and festivals, verdicts over disputes etc. It acted as an appellate court and dealt with serious breaches of social customs and punishes the offenders suitably by either excommunicating them or imposing a fine on them according to the nature and gravity of offences. The chief of the Panchayat was selected from the rank of the Mundas and was helped in discharging his duties by petty local officials called Pahan, Painbhara and Pandey etc.

But the British rule created the hitherto unknown class of zamindars in the tribal areas. The tribals were reduced to the position of tenants. The British also introduced Thekedars or contractors in the tribal areas. The zamindars and thekedars introduced the land rent in the tribal areas.

Following the introduction of the market economy, a class of traders also developed in the tribal areas. The tribal tenants had to pay the rent in cash. As they did not have cash with them, they had to borrow from the money-lenders. Hence, a class of money-lenders also came into being in these areas. The isolated tribal communities were connected to the outside world following the introduction of means of communication and transport. The self-sufficient tribal economy was converted into market economy. The customary system of justice was replaced by the new legal system. The tribals could not utilize the new legal system, as they were not educated & did not have money for the fees of the lawyers. The British brought a host of petty government officials and clerks in the tribal areas.

All these classes (zamindars, thekedars, traders, money-lenders, govt. officials, Christian missionaries) were not natives of these areas nor did they belong to tribal communities. Hence, they were considered outsiders (Dikus) by the tribals. These classes collaborated with the British administration in the process of exploitation and oppression of the tribals. The landlords' extracted exorbitant amount of rent from the tribals; evicted them from their land and extracted begar (forcible labour) from them. In case of defiance, the tribals were physically assaulted and often they were deprived of their belongings.

Reactionary and ill-conceived legislations like Criminal Tribes Act, 1871 made the conditions of tribes worse. By this Act many communities of craftsmen, traders and pastoralists were classified as criminal tribes. They were stated to be criminal by nature and birth. Once this Act came into force, these communities were expected to live in notified village settlements. They were not allowed to move out without a permit. The village police kept a continuous watch on them. By the establishment of Forest Department in 1864, Govt. Forest Act (1865) and Indian Forest Act in 1878 the British extended their control over all forests and declared forests as state property. Some forests were classified as reserved forests for they produced timber which the British wanted. In these forests people were not allowed to move freely, practice jhum cultivation, collect fruits and hunt animals. Many tribals were therefore forced to move to other areas in search of work and livelihood. They were recruited to work in tea plantations of Assam and coal mines of Jharkhand. They were recruited through contractors who paid them miserably low wages, and prevented them from returning home.

During the British rule in India, there has been encroachment on tribal hills and plain territories and oppression of the tribes by the aliens. Tribals by temperament are simple minded and nature-loving people. When they found their life-style and culture jeopardized by aliens' activities, they rose against the latter who were exploiting their economic resources including land, labour and forests.

The Chota Nagpur plateau, in the present Jharkhand state of India and a natural abode of many tribal communities from pre-historic times to Mughal period, witnessed many tribal movements in the colonial era. From 1830-1921, there were 4 major tribal movements in Chota Nagpur, viz. the Kol Rebellion (1831-32), Sardari Larai (1858-90), the Ulgulan or Birsa Munda movement (1895-1900) and Tana Bhagat movement (1914-25). Though these movements differ from each other in terms of ideology, structure and objective but the driving factors behind these movements are more or less the same. In order to highlight the diverse nature of tribal movements, K.S.Singh had divided them into two phases: 1765-1857 and 1857-1920. The first phase was primarily based on the nature of resistance against aliens or outsiders in both baronial and plebian sub-types whereas the second phase was agrarian and forest centered resistance which also included political issue, social reform and independence.

The earliest writings on tribes of Chota Nagpur were those of nineteenth century British administrators whose attention was drawn to tribal societies by the recurring tribal revolts. The tribal world, therefore, figured in official perceptions mainly as an adjunct to the counter- insurgency measures of the state. The perception gradually changed due to an improved understanding of tribal society. Tribes were then recognized as a worthwhile subject of study. In the 19th century a few British Administrators evinced keen interest in the ethnography and anthropology of tribal areas. W. W. Hunter (1868) in his *'Annals of Rural Bengal'* wrote about the tribes of Beerbhum and Santhal Paragana. Other important works included Col. E. T. Dalton's *'Descriptive Ethnology of Bengal'* (1872); H. S. Risley's *'Tribes and Castes of Bengal'* (1891); G. Archer's *'The Santhal Rebellion'* (1945).

F. B. Bradley–Birt in 1903 wrote *'Chota Nagpur: A Little-known Province of the Empire'* which is a detailed description of social, cultural and economic life of the various tribes residing in Chota Nagpur plateau.

The *Ranchi District Gazetteers* prepared by the efforts of T. S. Macpherson and M. G. Hallett throws light on physical aspects, history and people of Chota Nagpur and also give necessary statistical accounts. W. W. Hunter in vol. XVII of *Statistical Account of Bengal* had given a detailed description about aboriginal tribes of Chota Nagpur and Singhbhum district viz. the Kols, the Hos and the Mundas.

A parallel genre of literature on tribal studies relate to missionary accounts. Father Hoffmann's sixteen volumes of *'Encyclopedia Mundarika'* reveal the richness of Munda culture.

The 19th century British historians played a crucial role in provoking a nationalist reaction of writing tribal history. Sarat Chandra Roy, who is known as father of Indian ethnography, published many books on tribes of Chota Nagpur such as *'The Mundas and Their Country'* (1912), *'The Oraons of Chota Nagpur'* (1915), *'The Birhors, a Little Known Jungle Tribe of Chota Nagpur'* (1925) etc.

Kali Kinkar Datta's *'Santal Insurrection'* (1940) was one of the earliest discussions of tribal uprisings. Later K.K. Datta dealt with the tribal rebellions such as the Kol (that is the Munda and Larka Ho) uprising of 1831, the Santhal Hul of 1855 and Birsa Munda's Ulgulan revolt (1898-99) in detail in his *'History of the Freedom Movement in Bihar'* (1957) which has been published in 3 volumes. Datta considered the chief reason behind the rebellion to be the economic grievances of the people against their oppression and exploitation by the moneylenders and merchants.

Dhirendranath Baske ['*Saontal Ganasangramer Itihas*, 1976] likewise perceived the Santhal rebellion as primary a conscious political movement against colonial rule, challenging the point of view that considered the Santhal rebellion to be mere retaliation against the oppressions of Mahajans and traders rather than an anti-British movement. To Baske, the Kol and Santhal rebellions were in a sense political movements, as their objective was to establish their own raj, expelling outsiders, Indians as well as British.

Following in K. K. Datta's footsteps, three of his students, J. C. Jha, S. P. Sinha and K. S. Singh published monographs on similar movements in Chota Nagpur. In his work *'The Kol Insurrection'* (1964), Jha reiterated the argument that 'the tribal unrest of 1831-2 was a crude form of protest against the changes and the outside influences- a gesture of despair.' Jha says that the consequence of the revolt was the introduction of relief measures through Regulation XIII of 1833 whereby special rules were framed for the area which eased conflicts within tribal societies. Similarly he wrote in *'The Bhumij Revolt 1832-33'* the Bhumij revolt was 'a millenary or populist movement aimed at creating an ideal world' in which men would receive justice.

S. P. Sinha ('*Life and Times of Birsa Bhagwan*') and K. S. Singh ('*The Dust Storm and the Hanging Mist: A Study of Birsa Munda and his movement in Chota Nagpur, 1874-1971*') are a few studies dealing with Birsaite movements. Sinha argued that the tribal world, economically subordinate, was culturally inferior to that of the Hindus and Christians. Birsa Munda therefore had to borrow elements of the dominant culture to raise the status of the subordinate group. K.S. Singh, on the other hand, laid emphasis on economic issues, which undermined tribal agrarian structure. He observed, 'the transformation of the Mundari agrarian system into non-communal, feudal, zamindari or individual tenures was the key to agrarian disorders that climaxed into religious-political movements of Birsa.'

Three volumes on *Tribal Movements in India* edited by K. S. Singh are important contributions to the relatively scant literature on the subject. The first volume deals with the northeast frontier tribes, the second volume focuses on central and south India and the third volume confines itself to a survey of literature on tribal movements in different parts of the country.

The Subaltern Studies introduced a new trend in the historical research. Several volumes of 'Subaltern Studies' were published on Indian national movement under the editorship of Ranajit Guha in the 1980's. It brings to light the lower sections of Indian society hitherto neglected by historiography. Ranajit Guha, in the very first volume of Subaltern Studies, declared that "The historiography of Indian nationalism....been dominated by elitism – colonialist elitism and bourgeois- nationalist elitism." According to Guha, all type of elitist histories has one thing in common i.e. absence of the politics of the people from their accounts. In his essay, *"The prose of Counter Insurgency"*, Ranajit Guha launched a scathing attack on existing peasant and tribal histories in India for considering the tribal & peasant rebellions as 'purely spontaneous and unpremeditated affairs' and for ignoring the consciousness of the rebels. According to Guha, they all failed to acknowledge that there existed a parallel subaltern domain of politics which was not influenced by the elite politics and which possessed an independent, self-generating dynamics.

Among other recent writings on tribal history, Sanjukta Das Gupta has given a Historiographic overview of Peasant and tribal movements in Colonial Bengal in Sekhar Bandyopadhyay ed. *'Bengal: Rethinking History (Essays in Historiography)'*.

This book, using both conventional archival documents and non-traditional source materials like literature, oral testimonies and folklore, have tried to highlight various facets of tribal rebellions in Chota Nagpur such as the changing nature of the issues involved, participation, leadership and organization. While imperialist historians viewed them as barbaric, the nationalist historians placed tribal movements within the ambit of anti-colonial freedom struggle. The Marxist and Subaltern historians like A. R. Desai, Ranajit Guha and Gough treat tribal movements as part of peasant movements and described tribals as aboriginal kisans.

Further, tribal studies so far have tended to lay emphasis on the actual event of the revolt and studies on changing social formations have been comparatively few in number. Tribal societies and uprisings in Chota Nagpur, therefore, hold out real possibilities of interesting future research. The causes of their discontent, manner of their protests, different phases of their struggle, characteristics of their revolts, ideology of their leaders and other important aspects of the problem will be discussed in the work. Although a few research works are available on the subject but generally they have confined themselves to a particular revolt. Many of the tribal struggles have so far remained unexplored. I have tried to study the nature of all major tribal movements that occurred in Chota Nagpur in the period under study and have tried to fill in the various lacunas in this area.

OVERVIEW OF CHAPTERS

The book has been divided into five chapters besides the introduction and the conclusion.

Chapter I 'Chota Nagpur in the Early British period' narrates the historical journey of Chota Nagpur from the prehistoric era to the advent of the East India Company. The chapter traces the lineages of the Nagvanshi and the Chero dynasty of Chota Nagpur and discusses their relations with the East India Company and shows how the East India Company finally overtook the complete administration of Chota Nagpur in their hands. Lastly the chapter highlights the nature and significance of some of the major tribal uprisings during the Company rule viz. the Tamar rebellion of 1819-20, the Kol rebellion of 1831-32, the Bhumij revolt of 1832-33 and the Santhal Hul of 1855-57.

Chapter II 'Agrarian and Forest Movements' depicts how different legislations particularly the agrarian and forest laws of the colonial government affected the tribal communities of Chota Nagpur and discusses the resultant tribal movements that took place. Two such movements which had agrarian discontent as its root viz. the Sardar movement and the Kherwar movement have been carefully analyzed. Besides the grievances and discontent against forest laws have also been discussed in the chapter.

Chapter III 'Millenarian Movements' discusses another common theme in connection with tribal movements of Chota Nagpur i.e. the role of 'rebellious prophets' who launched 'messianic movements' promising their followers to drive out the outsiders and bring back a golden age. The Sapha Ho movement of the Santhals under Bhagirath Manjhi and Dubia Gossain and the Ulgulan movement of the Mundas under Birsa Munda were examples of religious revitalization movements that had a millenarian dream of establishing a Santhal Raj or Munda Raj respectively.

Chapter IV 'Going the Gandhian Way' traces the growth of nationalism among the tribes of Chota Nagpur after the visit of Gandhiji to Chota Nagpur in 1917. The chapter shows how the Adivasis were constantly supporting Gandhian ideology of non-violence, non-payment of taxation, temperance and vegetarianism, constructive programmes like khadi and charkha. The chapter discusses tribal movements of the Gandhian era viz. the Tana Bhagat movement and the Hari Baba movement. The chapter also tries to discover some unknown tribal freedom fighters of Chota Nagpur.

Chapter V 'Demand for Political Autonomy' discusses the demand for separate statehood that started after Bihar and Orissa were separated from Bengal in 1912 and became more profound after the formation of Adivasi Mahasabha in 1938. The Mahasabha wanted Chota Nagpur to be constituted as a separate province in order to improve the social, political and economic conditions of the tribals of Chota Nagpur. The chapter highlights the relations of Adivasi Mahasabha with the Congress and the Muslim League.

Finally, the conclusion has highlighted the main findings of the study.

CHAPTER I

CHOTA NAGPUR IN THE EARLY BRITISH PERIOD

The land of Chota Nagpur has been the silent spectator of the great upheavals and dynastic vicissitudes of Indian history, but unfortunately we do not find any systematic record of Chota Nagpur in ancient historical texts. Moreover the authenticity of the available literary sources is also not trustworthy as 'it has never been the Indian way to make a clearly defined distinction between myth, legend and history'.[1] Moreover, as Alberuni points out, 'the early Indian historians did not pay much attention to the historical order of things and were very careless in relating the chronological succession of things.'[2] However when we cautiously combine these literary, semi-historical and historical accounts with recent archaeological findings, and popular folklores among the tribes, our task would simplify to some extent.

TOPOGRAPHY AND THE EARLY ACCOUNTS

Archaeologists have unearthed many copper and stone artifacts at Ranchi, Palamau and Manbhum of the Chalcolithic period which are a silent proof that the area was inhabited for long. Although Vedic texts do not mention about Chota Nagpur perhaps because Aryans had not penetrated into this forest region for long, but inferences are found in Puranas esp. Vishnupurana and Vayupurana which has termed this region as *Murunda* or *Munda*. The Mahabharata mentions this region as *Pashubhumi* which was conquered by Bhim. It is a matter of debate among scholars whether the term '*Mundes*' used by Megasthenes, '*Mondes*' by Pliny and '*Mindala*' by Ptolemy may refer to Chota Nagpur or not.[3] The Allahabad Pillar inscription of Samudragupta also refer to the 'Murundas' and some scholars identify Murundas with the Mundas of Chota Nagpur.[4] However these are only speculations that rest merely on similarities of these words and may not be true.

The tribes of Chota Nagpur appear to have remained unmolested and outside the imperial administration of the Magadha Empire which reached its zenith during the rule of powerful Mauryans and the Guptas. This was most probably because of the inaccessible nature of the plateau which was walled off from the outside world by chains of wooded hills. Fa-Hien who went up to Gaya in the fifth century A.D. dared not to proceed further south to the Chota Nagpur plateau where the timid traveler remarked lions, tigers and wolves roam freely. Nor did Hiuen Tsang, who visited India in the seventh century, dare to enter this region, although he passed through its outskirts.[5] The long immunity from hostile disturbances enabled these tribes to build up their primitive social and administrative organizations.[6]

THE NAGVANSHIS OF CHOTA NAGPUR

It is a very difficult task to determine the date of the first ruler in Chota Nagpur. The origin of kingship is only supported by legends and folklore. Probably the Nagvanshis were the first who established their rule in this region. Till date four 'Nagvanshavalis' or 'Kursinama' are available to trace the genealogies of the Nagvanshi rulers of Chota Nagpur. The first Nagvanshavali was submitted by the 57th Maharaja Dripnath Sahi to the then Governor General of

Bengal Lord Cornwallis in 1787. The second was prepared by Beni Mahtha Ram in 1850 during the reign of Jagannath Shah. The third was prepared by Rakhal Das Haldar, the first Bhuinhari Commissioner and later on the Manager of Maharaja Raghunath Shah. It was published in "Man in India" in 1928 by S.C. Roy. The fourth Nagvanshavali is prepared by Man Gobinda Banerji in 1958-59. All these genealogies have slight variations in the chronology of rule.

A mythical story runs that Parikshit, son of Abhimanyu and the king of the Kuru kingdom after the Mahabharata war, was cursed by a sage's son to be bitten to death within a week by Takshaka, the king of the snakes. Unfortunately the curse proved to be true. Janmejaya, son of Parikshit, avenged his father's death by performing a Nagyagna to destroy the entire Nag-race. Pundarik Nag, son of Takshak, somehow managed to escape from the sacrifice and reached Kashi and married a Brahmin girl Parvati. The couple then moved towards Puri via the jungles of Jharkhand. Then, this region was under the supremacy of the Mundas. On the way Parvati gave birth to a son named Phani Mukut Rai. Soon the couple died and the infant was brought up by Madra Munda, the king of Mundas. Impressed by his administrative qualities Madra appointed Phani Mukut as his successor.[7]

This mythical story, when carefully analyzed, seems to convey the fact that the Naga tribe of Gandhar, when driven by the Aryans in the Vedic period, took shelter in the wild tracts of Jharkhand. Their leader was Pundarik Nag and his son, Phani Mukut Rai, established his supremacy over this region. The Mundas chose him as their ruler in 80 A.D. This view is supported by the Nagvanshavali of Beni Mahtha. Another plausible explanation is given by Dr. Lal

Chandra Churamani Nath Shahdeo. According to him, the Nagvanshis of Chotanagpur claimed their descent from the Shishunagvanshis of ancient Magadh, who migrated towards south and settled in Chotanagpur.[8]

However, according to the Ranchi district Gazetteer, the accession of Phani Mukut to the throne of Chota Nagpur took place somewhat around sixth century A.D.[9] This view is also accepted by Dr. S.K.Pandey who asserts that during the reign of Samudra Gupta (350-75 A.D.) the Nagvanshis had not settled in Chota Nagpur as Allahabad pillar inscription termed this region as Murunda (land of Mundas) and not as land of Nagas. Dr. Pandey asserts that the story of Nagyagna is perhaps associated with Samudragupta who after defeating a confederacy of Naga rulers in his second campaign of Aryavarta, invited them to participate in a sacrifice. A Nag ruler named Pundarik, kept himself aloof from this sacrifice and did not acknowledged the suzerainty of Samudragupta. Later the successors of Pundarik established their influence in Chota Nagpur and this is how the Nagvanshi rule in Chota Nagpur began.[10] This explanation seems to be the most appropriate in the light of present literary and archaeological findings.

We start getting information about Chotanagpur from the accounts of the court historians of Sultanate and Mughal rulers. However the word 'Jharkhand' was used in Sultanate period and the word 'Kokrah' was used in Mughal period for this region. Until the accession of Akbar, Chota Nagpur which was ruled by the Nagvanshis remained independent from the imperial authority of the Delhi Sultans. Afif tells us that Firoz Shah marched through Jharkhand against the Raja of Jajnagar (Odisha) but he didn't try to invade this region.[11]

The long splendid isolation of Chota Nagpur came to an end during the reign of Akbar. The Mughals came to know of this area as possessing diamond- mines (perhaps in the bed of river Sankh) which attracted their cupidity to this area.[12] Also, according to Abul Fazl, the Zamindar of Kokrah (as Chota Nagpur was called in Mughal times) was behaving presumptuously, relying on the difficulties of crossing an intervening mountain.[13] In 1585 A.D., Akbar sent a detachment under Shahbaz Khan Kambu and the Raja of Chota Nagpur was reduced to the position of vassal chief. Madhukar Rai[14], the Nagvanshi Raja submitted and agreed to pay malguzari (land revenue).

Again, during the reign of Jahangir, frequent campaigns were undertaken by the Mughal governors of Bihar against the Nagvanshi Raja of Chota Nagpur as he did not pay the promised annual tribute. It is now a determined fact that the contemporary ruler of Chota Nagpur during Jahangir's reign was Durjan Sal.[15] Jahangir describes in his memoirs "although the governors of Bihar frequently sent armies against him (Durjan Sal) and went there themselves, in consequent of the difficult roads and thickness of the Jungles they contented themselves with taking two or three diamonds and left him in his former condition."[16] Jahangir ordered Zafar Khan, the governor of Bihar in 1612 to invade Chota Nagpur and occupy the diamond mines of the region. However Zafar Khan was unsuccessful in this task and he was removed from his post.[17] Henceforth Jahangir appointed Ibrahim Khan as the governor of Bihar in 1615. Immediately after his appointment, Ibrahim Khan invaded Chota Nagpur and defeated Durjan Sal. As a reward, Jahangir raised the mansab of Ibrahim Khan to 4000 and the title of Fateh Jang was conferred on him.[18] All the diamond mines of the region came under the imperial control. Durjan Sal was send as a prisoner to the Gwalior Fort.

Durjan Sal remained in Mughal captivity for twelve years and released in 1627 by Jahangir and his territory was restored to him. Durjan Sal was henceforth to pay an annual tribute of Rs. 6000. After his release, Durjan Sal turned his capital Deosa into a magnificent fort city and introduced feudal system of administration.[19] It appears that henceforth the Nagvanshi rulers of Chota Nagpur, maintained cordial relations with the Mughal Empire but it is an astonishing fact that after Durjan Sal we practically get no reference of any other Nagvanshi ruler in later Mughal accounts of the period of Shah Jahan and Aurangzeb.[20]

THE CHEROS OF PALAMAU

Another ruling dynasty in Chota Nagpur in the eighteenth century, were the Cheros who had their stranglehold in the Palamau region. The Cheros have established small principalities in Western Bihar (Shahabad, Saran, Champaran and Muzaffarpur regions of Bihar) in the first quarter of the 12th century itself following the decline of the Pal dynasty. The Afghan sources mention that the Cheros were quite powerful in Shahabad region.[21] The author of Tarikh-i-Sher Shahi writes that Maharata Chero had become so powerful that Sher Shah sent Khawas Khan to punish him but before the campaign could be affectively taken up, Khawas Khan was called back to take part in the battle of Chausa against Humayun. Therefore the campaign against Chero chief was temporarily suspended but it was soon resumed after the battle of Bilgram. Khawas Khan easily defeated and killed Maharata Chero. Contemporary Afghan sources have mentioned that Sher Shah undertook Chero campaign "in order to get possession of a white elephant called Syam Chander." The Chero chief was besieged and compelled to surrender the elephant. Prof. K.R.Qanungo ridicules this story and asserts that the actual cause of invasion was from a strategic point of view as the territory governed by Maharata Chero lied between Rohtas and Bengal.[22]

During Mughal period, the Chero chieftaincies of Bihar declined and the Chero chief of Palamau in the Chotanagpur region emerged as the most powerful ruler among the Cheros. The founder of Chero dynasty of Palamau was Bhagwant Rai. He was the Chero chief of Chainpur (Bhojpur) and took service under the Raksel Rajput chief, Man Singh of Palamau, and after murdering his master founded his own kingdom in around 1572. Thereafter we have no account of any other Chero ruler until Anant Chero a contemporary of Emperor Akbar. Akbar sent Raja Man Singh, the governor of Bihar to reduce him to submission around 1590-91. Anant Chero offered stiff resistance but he was defeated and thereafter Palamau was also brought under Mughal administration.

An important outcome of the Mughal inroads into Chotanagpur was the end of its long-splendid isolation. Both the Nagvanshi and the Chero rulers became vassal chiefs of Mughal emperor. They adopted the administrative and architectural ideas of the Mughals. For instance when Durjan Sal returned from Mughal captivity he built magnificent forts and temples at Doisa. Moreover, people from Northern India came to Chota Nagpur in large numbers and lands were assigned to them in lieu of military services. Brahmins were also encouraged by lavish grants of villages to settle here and to aid in civilizing it in their own ways.[23] However, the aboriginal tribes resisted against this large scale intrusion of the outsiders into this region.

Chotanagpur in Medieval period (Source- B. Virottam *'Jharkhand: Itihaas evam Sanskriti'* (in Hindi), Patna, 2001)

By the time the British arrived at Chotanagpur, the internal organization of the entire area was in widespread chaos, confusion and disaster. Factors contributing to this dismal state of affairs were the frequent incursions of the Marathas, regular hostilities between local chiefs and rival Jagirdars, as well as the uprisings of the aboriginal population in protest against the presence of the Hindus and Muslim communities from Bengal and Bihar, who were gradually encroaching upon their time-honored rights over land and forests. The region had become reduced to a ruinous condition. To exacerbate the situation further were the age old agrarian problems and the specific question over land question.[24] At this juncture, the Mughal emperor Shah Alam II on August 12, 1765 A.D. assigned the Diwani or revenue administration of Bengal, Bihar and Orissa to the English East India Company for an annual payment of 2,600,000 rupees.[25] Chota Nagpur technically being a part of the Subah of Bihar came under the control of the East India Company and the Nagvanshi and Chero rulers of Chota Nagpur were, thus, considered liable to the payment of revenue to the East India Company.

However, the claims of the Company to get the tribute of Chota Nagpur as the Diwan of Bengal, Bihar and Orissa had no legal basis. *Firstly* because the Nagvanshis of Ranchi and the Cheros of Palamau represented the old class of Hindu Rajas who had established themselves in their territories even before the Mughal conquest of Bihar and Bengal. They were *de facto* rulers in their territories, subject to the payment of a tribute or land tax to the representative of the Emperor. Therefore, they were, in fact, semi-subdued chiefs of ancient standing, who had not been brought under the administrative control of the Mughal Government.[26]*Secondly* because they had held their princely courts, administered justice in their own territories and maintained their own bands of armed followers. They never paid tribute except an army advanced against them. *Thirdly* they never deemed it necessary to secure an official recognition of their succession as was the case with most of the other chiefs of Mughal India directly under Mughal control.[27] And *finally* during the years immediately preceding the grant of Diwani of the East India Company, these areas were considered almost lost to the Mohammadan authorities at Patna.[28]

During the early years of the East India Company, the officials of the Company had very vague ideas regarding the geographical location of these areas and up till the middle of the 18th century the country between Sherghati and Pachet was almost like a blank on the map.[29] The revenue map drawn by Mohammad Reza Khan at the orders of the East

India Company, had excluded these territories from the assessed territory in 1765. Thus, factually the Rajas of the Chota Nagpur plateau including those of Palamau, Ramgarh and Chota Nagpur, amongst others, should have remained as independent states.[30]

ANGLO- NAGVANSHI RELATIONS

The British entry into Chota Nagpur was clearly a case of intervention in the internal affairs of independent chieftains taking advantage of their numerous difficulties, and it was a measure of political expediency based purely on military and economic considerations.[31] The Maratha menace to Chota Nagpur and Palamau also posed a grave danger to the East India Company's possessions in Bihar. Moreover, Palamau had become the refuge of those Zamindars of South Bihar who chose to defy the authority of the East India Company. Family dissensions, inroads of neighbouring territories, and esp. of the Marathas and lack of military preparedness, all these factors goaded the authorities of East India Company at Patna to try to secure the annexation of Chota Nagpur and Palamau and to bring the Nagvanshis and the Cheros under its direct control.[32]

The first to fall in the vicious rat trap of the English Company was the Nagvanshi ruler of Chota Nagpur- Drip Nath Shahi who probably ruled between 1761 to1787. His dominion extended over the entire territory constituting the South Chotanagpur division- Ranchi, Khunti, Gumla, Lohardaga districts and also up to Latehar district (which was known as Tori Pargana) at present. However his relations with the chiefs of Ramgarh, Palamau and Singhbhum were not in good terms owing to his policy of unrestrained expansionism.

Therefore, Drip Nath Shah befriended the officers of the Company and actively supported Capt. Jacob Camac (the commander of 24ᵗʰ Native Infantry Battalion of Patna) in his Palamau expedition by procuring provisions and other necessities. Drip Nath Shah also went personally to congratulate Camac for his Palamau victory and met him in his camp at Satbarwa. He acknowledged himself as a vassal of the Company and agreed to pay annual revenue of twelve thousand rupees, besides furnishing help against the Marathas. The agreement was cemented by Drip Nath Shah exchanging his turban with Camac's cap. According to Jacob Camac this agreement with the Nagvanshi Raja was significant because under the changed circumstances, there remained no route open to the Marathas to invade Bengal and South Bihar, except through Orissa and the west and also he could easily reduce Mukund Singh of Ramgarh with the assistance of the Nagvanshi Raja.

At the recommendation of Camac, Patna Council concluded a formal settlement with Drip Nath Shah in August 1771 in which revenue was fixed at Rs. 36001 for three years (1771 to 1773 A.D.), inclusive of '*nuzrana, salami* and other *abwabs.*' However Drip Nath Shah was never punctual in payment of revenue to the Company and hence Patna Council detached Lt. Richard Fennell in 1773 to subdue him and pay the arrears. Drip Nath Shah paid the arrear revenue to Camac in the beginning of 1774. However, for a ruler like Drip Nath, whose territory was a forested area where there was little improvement in agriculture and where his vassals viz. the chiefs of Panch Pargana of Ranchi district (namely Silli, Bundu, Baranda, Rahe and Tamar) were not paying tribute to him regularly, it became increasingly difficult to pay such a large amount of revenue and hence the revenue from Chota Nagpur was constantly in arrears.[33]

ANGLO- CHERO RELATIONS

Initially, the Company's authorities at Calcutta hesitated in the subjugation of Palamau, the stranglehold of the Chero rulers. They had instructed the Patna Council to abstain from the use of force for the reduction of Palamau. However the political chaos and confusion prevailing in Palamau gave impetus to the designs of the East India Company. Jai Krishna Rai (1722-1770), the Chero ruler of Palamau was not in good terms with his Diwan Amar Singh and got his son Sainath Singh murdered. The family of Sainath led by his nephew Jainath Singh soon avenged his death and Jai Krishna Rai was killed in a skirmish at Chetma in 1770. Chitrajit Rai (1770-1771) was declared the next ruler with Jainath Singh as his Diwan.

When Palamau was facing this state of civil war, the British had arrived at the doorstep of Chota Nagpur and they decided to support the cause of Gopal Rai, the grandson of late Chero chief Jai Krishna Rai and place him on throne. However, the Company first decided to settle the dispute through negotiations. On 9 Jan 1771, the Patna Council sent Ghulam Hussain Khan to meet Diwan Jainath Singh and persuade him to surrender Palamau fort peacefully. When the Company did not receive any reply from Jainath within 10 days, they gave orders to Capt. Camac to attack Palamau. Capt. Camac occupied the fort on March 20, 1771. Gopal Rai was made the Raja and a settlement was concluded with him in July 1771 whereby he agreed to pay annual revenue of Rs. 12000 though the Palamau fort was retained by the Company.

Thus, by July 1771, the East India Company's authority was established practically over the whole of Palamau and the Chero ruler had turned as its vassal.

The subjugation of the Chota Nagpur was thus complete and the Rajas became tenants of their kingdoms, paying various amounts of money to the British to retain their kingship.

TRIBAL REVOLTS IN CHOTANAGPUR UNDER THE COMPANY RULE:

In the process of colonization, the East India Company had to face many tribal uprisings. The prevailing political and economic situation added fuel to the fire. Firstly due to repeated Maratha incursions, Chota Nagpur was in a state of anarchy and therefore its aboriginal residents rose in revolt. Secondly, the Zamindars of Chota Nagpur such as Jainath Singh of Palamau, Drip Nath Shah of Chota Nagpur proper, Mukund Singh of Ramgarh and Jagannath Dhal of Dhalbhum who were now dependent on the Company for their existence, were secretly supporting these tribal uprisings. Thirdly, the region had to face the adversities of repeated famines in 1770, 1777 and again in 1800 and therefore, its inhabitants being unable to bear the burden of increased taxation took up arms. Lastly, the aboriginals were exploited by the landlords, moneylenders, administrators, police, indigo planters and traders whom they called as 'dikus'.[34] Some of the major tribal uprisings of Chotanagpur during the Company rule are:

1. Tamar Rebellion of 1819-20

In 1817 Chotanagpur was brought under the direct administration of East India Company as part of Ramgarh district which meant that that the feudal authority of the Nagvanshi rulers came to an end.[35] the extension of the company's direct administration on Chotanagpur failed to have the desired effect. The inhabitants, in general, were dissatisfied by this action of the Government.[36] The main cause of dissatisfaction was that the subordinate officers, appointed by the Government, were either Hindus or Muslims. They were aliens, ignorant of the language, culture and customs of Chotanagpur. These alien officers had no sympathy for the tribals. So, the latter felt persecuted in their own country.[37]

Moreover, since the introduction of police system by the British and the appointment of the first 'Political Agent to Government in South Bihar and the recently ceded districts adjacent to that province' in 1819, the outsiders had been pouring in Chotanagpur as police darogas, court amlas and 'abkari' farmers, who did not have the slightest knowledge of the language, customs and sentiments of these people. Consequently they used tricks and fraudulent methods to exploit these simple aborigines. Thus there was smouldering discontent among the aborigines against the infiltration of the foreigners.[38]

The immediate cause of this rebellion was that in 1818 a religious mendicant, named Narain Bhatta Brahmachari, persuaded Maharaja Govind Nath Shah to believe that an old woman, Adhar Dai, had destroyed his children by witchcraft. On this suspicion Adhar Dai and her family were murdered by the Maharaja. This event made the tribals violent and the result was the insurrection of 1819-20.[39] The insurrection broke out in Tamar Pargana in August 1819 against the jagirdars and thekedars and was led by two Munda leaders Rughdeo and Konta. Major Roughsedge arrived with a Ramgarh battalion to quell the uprising. Both Rughdeo and Konta were arrested and peace was restored.[40]

2. Kol Rebellion of 1831-32

In 1822, after the death of Raja Govind Deo, his nineteen year old son, Raja Jagannath Sahi Deo became the Raja of Chota Nagpur. Cuthbert, the officiating Collector, rightly predicted, on this occasion that "the young Raja probably like his father will be a mere cipher in his Raj".[41] Raja Jagannath incurred huge debts to the Sikh horse dealers and Mohammedan cloth merchants, and so was obliged to lease out villages to collect taxes for a specified time. These came to be known as thekedars, who practiced extortion on the villagers by violence and fraud.[42] They always tried to squeeze as much as possible from the ryots in the shape of rents, abwabs and salamis. The tribals had too much to endure. The result was the general revolt in 1831-32.[43]

The immediate reason was the following. The brother of Maharaja Jagannath Sahi Deo made grants of villages in Sonepur to certain Mohammedans, Sikhs and Hindus; and so the mundas and mankis (village headmen) not only lost their ancestral villages but the foreigners seduced their women and sisters. The Mundas could not bear this type of oppression and so they decided to 'burn, plunder, murder and loot' their oppressors.[44]

The insurrection started on 11th December 1831, when a party of Kols carried out about two hundred heads of cattle from a small village Kochang of Sonepur. The movement spread from the present district of Ranchi to Singhbhum, Manbhum, Hazaribagh and Palamau. Captain Impey went to quell the uprising and Sir Thomas Wilkinson followed him later on.[45]

There was a Government inquiry into the insurrection. Major Sutherland, the private Secretary to the Vice President in Council, in a report of the year 1832 gave the following reasons. The tribals hated the Hindus and Mohammedans. The Hindus were mostly traders and moneylenders who made enormous profits while the Mohammedans levied usurious interests. The tribals were hardly able to get out of the clutches of either because the 'interlopers' were backed by the police and the court.[46]

Mr. Blunt, who had lived in Chota Nagpur (1805) and was later a member of Governor-General's Council, wrote in his minutes a detailed account of the cases of the insurrection. He pointed out that dispossession of the mankis and mundas of Sonepur, Tamar, Sillie, Bundu and the adjacent Parganas from the hereditary land was the cause of unrest. To restore and permanently secure tranquility it was necessary, he said, to reinstate the hereditary proprietors who have been dispossessed from their land in Chota Nagpur.[47]

The rising of the Kols in 1831-32 has been variously described by different writers. O'Malley calls it the 'Kol rebellion' in which the Mundas and the Oraons 'rose en masse' and were joined by the Hos, the Cheros and the Kharwars.[48] On the other hand, Bradley Birt refers to it as 'the Kol Mutiny'.[49] Thornton described the risings as an orgy of mutual slaughter in which "the hand of every man is against his neighbour."[50] J.C. Jha calls the disturbances as the "Kol Insurrection".[51] J. Reid also gives the same title to this explosion.[52]

Therefore, the Kol rebellion was against the agrarian system, debt laws and the new judicial and revenue regulations (e.g. excise duties, tributary payments) etc. and 'the influx of hordes of middlemen'. This rising made the government aware of 'the necessity of radical reforms in the administration and after the suppression of the revolt every cause of discontent of the Adivasis was sought to be removed by the reforms in administrative, judicial, police, revenue and debt laws and restrictions were imposed on transfer or mortgage of landed property to avoid fraud by middlemen.' A big administrative change from Regulation to Non-Regulation system of government took place after the insurrection was suppressed.[53]

3. BHUMIJ REVOLT (1832-33)

Immediately after the Kol rebellion, the Bhumijs of Manbhum under the leadership of Ganga Narain revolted against the new diwan of Barabhum – Madhab Singh in 1832. The rebels looted the munsif's cutcheries, set fire to the police stations, destroyed government offices and killed Diwan Madhab Singh for his 'diku' like behaviour. Initially it all centered on the disputed succession in the Barabhum zamindar family. The Bhumijs were dissatisfied with the British court's order that the eldest born of even the second wife of a zamindar should succeed.

The extension of Permanent Settlement and the Cornwallis Code to these undeveloped hilly tract without taking any note of tribal interests, needs and customs, did great harm to the tribesmen. Moreover, the Ghatwals, who were traditional policemen, lost their land grants because they were replaced by corrupt non-tribal policemen. Widespread dissatisfaction over their loss of land and excessive taxes led the adivasi people to rally behind Ganga Narain. He was able to capture Barabhum from the British with the help of some three thousand Bhumij rebels and conferred on himself the title of raja. The British forces succeeded in bringing the situation under control in November- December 1832. When faced with British troops from all sides, Ganga Narain fled to Singhbhum along with some of his followers where he was ultimately killed in February 1833.[5]

4. SANTHAL HUL (1855-57)

The Santhal rebellion of 1855-57 was not restricted only to Santhal Parganas but it reverberated as far as Birbhum, Bankura and Hazaribagh. The main leaders of this insurrection were Sidhu, Kanhu, Chand and Bhairav of village Bhagnadihi. It had its origin in the economic grievances of the Santhals, due to the oppressions and frauds committed to those simple minded people by the Bengali and upcountry merchants and moneylenders. The extortions of those merchants and Mahajans had become awful, and they had amassed large fortunes within an incredibly short period by recurring cash and grains from the Santhals through various obnoxious ways.[55]

According to the settlement officer H. Macpherson, the deeper cause of the insurrection was 'the Santhal yearning for independence, a dream of the ancient days when they had no overlords'.[56] The Santhals wanted to drive out the British and the dikus and establish an independent Santhal Raj. The insurgents used bows, poisoned arrows, axes and swords. In Hazaribagh, the 40th Regiment was sent for suppressing the rebellion and it was brutally suppressed. Santhal villages were raided and their property destroyed.[57]

After the suppression of the rebellion an enquiry headed by Ashley Eden was set up to look into the grievances of the Santhals. As a consequence, a lot of administrative measures were taken by East India Company such as introduction of the Act XXXVII of 22 December 1855. This act formed the territory in and around Damin-i-Koh into a separate non-regulation district called Santhal Parganas. It was placed under the direct control of the Commissioner of Bhagalpur subsequently. However, due to the complaints from European indigo planters and zamindars, the Act was nullified and the district was shrunk into a smaller area under the Act X of 1857. The new district created from the Santhali areas of Bhagalpur and Birbhum districts was divided into four sub-districts – Dumka, Deoghar, Godda and Rajmahal – and placed under a deputy commissioner and four assistant commissioners with civil and criminal jurisdiction. The administrative measures also included an amendment of the existing land law by which unrestricted purchase and sale of land was declared illegal in the 52 moujas of the newly created district.[58]

However these early uprisings were in fact not against the Government, but mainly against the local Rajas and the Zamindars. But as the British wanted to consolidate their power in Chotanagpur, they had to interfere and they naturally sided with the local Rajas and landlords because they were influential people and their cooperation would have proved quite beneficial for the alien rulers. It was much due to the

British power that all these rebellions which occurred in Chotanagpur before the outbreak of the Revolt of 1857 were crushed with iron hands. For instance Bishun Manki, Rudan Munda and Kanda Munda, the leaders of Tamar uprisings of 1807 and 1812 were arrested and put behind the bars.[59]

The Tribals of Chotanagpur and the 1857 Uprising: The 1857 uprising has largely been studied in terms of the participation in it of sepoys, and the peasants who saw in this event an opportunity to ventilate their grievances and assert their rights, led by feudal aristocracy which saw its privileges threatened or taken away. The tribals are not mentioned as such in the chronicles of the uprising. While the tribes and the peasants demonstrated many similarities in their response to the uprising, there were also significant differences emanating from their social structures and political systems. There was in fact a plurality of responses. The tribes were not only fighting the colonial rulers, the enemy outside, but they also tried to settle scores with the enemies within, the exploiters, the moneylenders, the rivals in regional power structure and so on.

The narrative of the events of revolt of 1857 showed that the movement at Chotanagpur was of a very different nature from a mere mutiny of the sepoys. People belonging to all walks of life took active part in the movement. The civil population led by their Zamindars and Jagirdars had taken to arms. Important leaders who revolted against the British were Pandey Ganpat Nath Roy, Thakur Vishwanath Shahi, Vishwanath Dubey, Mahesh Narain Shahi, Tikait Omrao Singh, Shaikh Bhikari, Brij Bhushan Singh, Chana Singh, Ramlal Singh, Vijoy Ram Singh, Bahoran Singh, Zamadar Qurban Ali, Thakur Kishan Dayal Singh etc.[60]

In the backdrop of these revolts, some administrative, political and socio-economic reforms were also carried out from time to time. An era of subjugation and experimentation in administration commenced. It took shape in four phases. In the first phase (1767-80), the British administration was concerned more for extracting taxes and revenue than for anything else. In 1774, Chota Nagpur along with Palamau and Ramgarh was placed under a Military Collector who was directly under the control of Governor-General and his council. The Military Collector was concerned more with the settlement and realization of revenues and with bringing the country into a proper state of subjection. Capt. Camac was assigned with this duty. The internal administration of Chota Nagpur was left entirely in the hands of the local Rajas and Company made little interference on their part.

In the second phase (1780-1833), Military administration was abolished and the Company started administration in Chota Nagpur through civilians. The Ramgarh Hill Tract District with a civil administrator was formed in 1780. The newly formed district comprised the present districts of Hazaribagh, Palamau, and parts of the present districts of Gaya, Manbhum and Mungher, while '...Chota Nagpur proper under its own tributary chief owned a vague allegiance to East India Company and formed but a nominal part of this huge district.' Mr. Chapman was the first officer to be vested with this triple appointment of Judge, Magistrate and Collector. On 4 June 1809, six Police Thanas were established and this marks the beginning of the death keel of the Raja's feudal authority and growing Company control on administration.

In the third phase (1833-54), the Ramgarh Hill Tract area was designated the South West Frontier Agency in 1833, which was a 'non-regulation province' rather than a district, with its civil headquarters at Ranchi. A court was established at Lohardaga. The zamindari police system was introduced. At the Sadar district Police stations were established and maintained at Government expense. Zamindari stations were established at Palkote where the Maharaja then had his seat. Subsequently other police stations were opened at Govindpur, Bundu, Tamar, Sillie, Barway and Banta Hajam, though 'in Chota Nagpur it [zamindari police] amounted to nothing less than the appointment of wolf as shepherd.' In 1842, the administrative headquarters was transferred from Lohardaga to Ranchi.

In the fourth phase (1854-1857), the South West Frontier Agency was abolished and Chotanagpur division was created in 1854 and was composed of five districts – Hazaribagh, Ranchi, Palamau, Manbhum and Singhbhum. This was administered as a non-regulation province under a Commissioner reporting to the Lieutenant Governor of Bengal.

NOTES AND REFERENCES

1. Winternitz, *A History of Indian Literature*, Vol. II, Calcutta, 1933, p.208.

2. Sachau, *Alberuni's India*, Vol. II, London, 1910, pp.10-11.

3. Banerji, Man Gobinda. "The Name Chota Nagpur", *Journal of the Bihar and Orissa Research Society*, Vol. XXVI, 1940, pp.189-223.

4. Pandey, Hari Shankar. "Early Political History of Chotanagpur in Historical Perspective", *Proceedings of the Indian History Congress*, Vol. 61, 2000, pp.169-173.

5. Gautam, Ambrish. "Chota Nagpur- An Untold History: A Socio-Historical Analysis", *Anthropology*, Vol.5, 2017, pp.1-18.

6. Roy, S.C. *The Mundas and their Country*, 1912, Calcutta, p.115.

7. Roy, S.C. ibid, pp.135-140.

8. Sinha, Sudha. *The Nagvanshis of Chotanagpur*, 2001, New Delhi, pp.7-8.

9. Macpherson, T.S. and Hallett, M.G. *Bihar and Orissa District Gazetteers: Ranchi*, Patna, 1917, p.24.

10. Pandey, S.K. *History and Culture of Jharkhand*, Agra, 2020, p.105.

11. Afif, *Tarikh-i-Firoz Shahi*, tr. Wilayat Husain, Calcutta, 1890, pp.172-179.

12. Sudha Sinha, op. cit., pp. 36-39.

13. Abul Fazl, *Akbarnama* (tr. Beveridge), vol. III, p.722. See also Shah Nawaz Khan & Abdul Hayy, *Maathir-ul-Umara* (tr. Beveridge), vol. II, Calcutta, 1952, p. 736.

14. Abul Fazl and Shah Nawaz Khan had named this ruler as Madhu Singh. The *Nagvanshavali* of Beni Mahtha also had mentioned a Nagvanshi ruler named Madhukar Shah. So, we can conclude that Madhukar Shah was the ruler of Chota Nagpur at the time of the Mughal invasion of 1585. (Sudha Sinha, op. cit. p.37).

15. Although according to the *Nagvanshavali* Durjan Sal ruled from 1565 to 1606 and was the predecessor of Madhukar Shah but this is not true as it is evident from the Mughal accounts that Madhukar Shah was a contemporary of Akbar and Durjan Sal was of Jahangir.

16. *Tuzuk-i-Jahangiri* (translated by Rogers and Beveridge), vol. I, p. 315.

17. Mirza Nathan, *Baharistan-i-Ghaybi* (tr. Borah), vol. I, 1936, Assam, pp.257-58. According to Mirza Nathan, the campaign led by Zafar Khan was against Barisal. Barisal was the father of Durjan Sal who succeeded Madhukar Shah in circa 1600 and died in 1614 after a reign of 14 years. (H. Blockmann, "Notes from Mohammadan Historians on Chutia Nagpur, Pachet and Palamau", *JASB*, 1871, p.115.)

18. *Tuzuk-i-Jahangiri* (translated by Rogers and Beveridge), vol. I, p. 316.

19. Sudha Sinha, op. cit., pp. 38-41. See also Lal Pradumn Singh, *Nagvansh*, Lucknow, 1951, part II, p. 77.

20. Ansari, T.H. *Mughal Administration and the Zamindars of Bihar*, 2019, p.168.

21. Singh, K.S. *The Cheros* (Ms). *The Comprehensive History of Bihar*, vol. II Pt. I edited by S.H.Askari and Q.Ahmad, p.259. See also Ansari, op. cit. pp. 135-137.

22. Qanungo, K.R. *Shershah and His Times*, 1965, p. 181.

23. Virottam, Balmukund. *The Nagbanshis and the Cheros*, 1972, New Delhi, p.21.

24. Jha, Seema Rajiv (2017). *The history of the Jharkhand movement 1912-2000: Socio-Cultural and political implications* (Doctoral thesis, University of Mumbai).

25. Hunter, W.W. *Bengal Ms. Records*, Vol. I, London, 1894, p.17.

26. Virottam, Balmukund, op. cit., 1972, pp. 71-72.

27. Hunter, W.W., op. cit., p. 33.

28. Fifth Report, Vol. II, pp. 441-442.

29. Datta, K.K. *Bengal Subah*, Vol. I, p. 394.

30. Goswami, P. *Untold Story of Chota Nagpur: Its journey with the Colonial Army 1767-1947*, 2020, Chennai, p.16.

31. Virottam, Balmukund, op. cit., 1972, p.72.

32. *Ibid*, p.198.

33. Bose, N.K. The Structure of Hindu Society, p.49.

34. Virottam, Balmukund. *Jharkhand: Itihas evam Sanskriti*, Bihar Hindi Granth Academy, Patna, 2001, pp.131-133.

35. Roy, S.C. op. cit. p. 190.

36. Virottam, Balmukund, op. cit., 1972, p. 176.

37. Peter Tete, S.J. *A Missionary Social Worker in India*, Roma, 1984, p. 8.

38. Jha, J.C. "The Kol Rising of Chotanagpur (1831-33): Its Causes", *Proceedings of Indian History Congress*, vol. 21 (1958), pp. 440-446.

39. Sinha, Sudha. op. cit. p. 78.

40. Peter Tete, S.J. op. cit. p. 9.

41. Cuthbert to Govt., 1 August 1822, Bengal Revenue Consultation, 28 of 8 August 1822 (59/21) Quoted in Sudha Sinha, op. cit. p. 81.

42. Hoffmann, J.B. Encyclopedia Mundarika, 1932, vol. V, p. 1444.

43. Roy, S.C. op. cit. p. 201.

44. Peter Tete, S.J. op. cit. p. 10.

45. Kumar, Anil. "An Unknown Chapter of Kol-Insurrection", Proceedings of Indian History Congress, vol. 62(2001), pp. 621-626.

46. Roy, S.C. op. cit. p. 209.

47. Ibid, p. 211.

48. O' Malley, L.S.S. *History of Bengal, Bihar and Orissa under British Rule*, Calcutta, 1925, p. 689.

49. Bradley Birt, F.B. *Chotanagpur: A little known Province of the Empire*, London, 1903, p. 92.

50. Thornton, E. *The History of the British Empire in India*, vol. V, London, 1841-43, p. 203.

51. Jha, J.C. *The Kol Insurrection of Chotanagpur*, Calcutta, 1964.

52. Reid, J. *Final Report on the Survey and Settlement Operations in the District of Ranchi, 1902-1910*, Calcutta, 1912, p. 22.

53. Jha, J.C. "The Kol Rising of Chotanagpur (1831-33): Its Causes", *Proceedings of Indian History Congress*, vol. 21 (1958), pp. 440-446.

54. Ghosh, A. "Jharkhand Movement in West Bengal", *Economic and Political Weekly*, vol. 28, Jan. 1993, pp. 121-127.

55. Dutta, K.K. *Anti- British Plots and Movements*, Meenakshi Prakashan: Meerut, 2006, pp. 46-47.

56. Areeparampil, M. *Struggle for Swaraj*, TRTC, Chaibasa, 2002, p. 144.

57. De, Debasree. *Gandhi and Adivasis*, Manohar: New Delhi, 2022, pp.22-24.

58. Xalxo, Abha. "The Great Santhal Insurrection (Hul) of 1855-56", *Proceedings of the Indian History Congress*, vol. 69, 2008, pp. 732-55.

59. Chaudhary, Prasanna Kumar and Srikant. *Bihar-Jharkhand me Mahayuddha* (in Hindi), Patna, 2008, pp.275-76.

60. Roy Chaudhary, P.C. *Bihar mein 1857*, pp.107-110.

CHAPTER II

AGRARIAN AND FOREST MOVEMENTS

Land, water and forest (Jal, Jangal and Jameen) which together constitute the surroundings in the nature are not only the traditional key sources of livelihood of the tribal communities, but their culture, lifestyle, customs, rites-rituals, folkways and even their whole life vibrates accordingly. They worship these natural constituents and ecosystem's surrounding bodies like the hill (Buru Bonga), the Sun (Sing Bonga), village spirit (Hatu Bonga) as their gods and goddesses. Each tribal community derive their lineage (gotra or kili) in special relationship with environment like ekka (turtle), toppo (woodpecker), kerketta (quail), lakra (tiger), xess (rice or paddy), kujur (a creeper), panna (iron), soreng (rock), tete (a bird). Therefore obviously, intrusions or interferences of the outer world in to their lives had affected their entire traditional, social, cultural and natural resources based economy in very painful manner.

In spite of several scholarly works produced by the ethnographers, anthropologists and historians on the tribal movements from the Kol Insurrection in Chotanagpur to Tana Bhagat movement (1914-21), there is still a crucial gap in the study. There is hardly any serious work which exclusively narrates these movements in the background of colonial expansion in the Chotanagpur tract and links them up with the expropriation of the surplus generated through the imposition of land rent, its exorbitant enhancement and control of the forest wealth by colonial authorities, and at times their collaborators such as the land- grabbers, the Mahajans and the moneylenders.[1]

The census operation, enumeration of the houses, preparation of the records of land rights, fixation of land tax and categorisation of the land in various categories, all such measures and enactments of various laws in the 1860s and 1870s aimed at imposition of land tax and fixing enhanced rent so as to accumulate surpluses for furtherance of the interest of the British empire. This chapter carefully analyses how different legislations particularly the agrarian and forest laws affected the tribal communities of Chotanagpur and discusses the resultant tribal movements that took place.

STRUCTURAL CHANGES IN THE LAND ADMINISTRATION IN COLONIAL ERA

On April 15, 1858, Lala Lokenath Sahi, a local zamindar and Sub- Assistant Commissioner was deputed to prepare a register of all the ancestral land of the tribals. But with his death on August 13, 1862, the survey stopped.[2]

With a view to an authoritative settlement of the title to *Bhuinhari* lands the *Chota Nagpur Tenures Act* (Act II of 1869) was passed by the Bengal Council on July 26, 1869. According to this Act provisions were made for the demarcation, mapping and registration of the bhuinhari and private lands. Under the Act, special Commissioners were appointed, who had power to survey and demarcate the privileged lands of the tenants (bhuinhari) and the landlords (manjhihas). The manjhihas lands correspond to the nij-jote lands of the zamindars in Bengal, with this difference that they are held to be at the "absolute disposal" of the landlords, and occupancy rights cannot accrue in them in any circumstances whatsoever. The proprietor of Manjhihas land was entitled to get usually 12 days labour from his tenants for its cultivation. Such compulsory labour without payment by tenants was called Bethbegari.[3]

The first Special Commissioner appointed for this purpose was Babu Rakhal Das Haldar. The operations, which commenced on 1st April 1869 was not concluded till 31st March 1880. The enquiries extended to 2482 villages in Ranchi district, and the total cost amounted to Rs. 269,887.[4]

When the settlement began the zamindars started rumours that the Government wanted to know the exact amount of the bhuinhari fields and to exact heavy rent for each plot. The zamindars procured copies of the declaration of lands in the villages, and knew how much the Mundas had declared. Thus they acquired the undeclared bhuinhari fields by their clever tricks. The court and Settlement Commissioner also took for granted that all the rest of the undeclared land belonged to the zamindar. The Munda then had to file an expensive civil suit to prove that the fields belonged to him. In order to pay the court fees the Tribal needed cash, which he always lacked. He was forced to go to the moneylender to get a loan at an exorbitant rent varying from 15 to 75 percent. Since he had no documentary title for his lands the law suit was always against him. By then he was a ruined man. He had no other choice than to leave his ancestral land and work as indentured labour in mines, factories or tea plantations of Assam.[5]

The greatest defect of the Bhuinhari settlement of 1869 lay in the fact that the Government had acted without hearing and examining question as to who was in fact the real and ultimate owner of the Mundari village community. It did not pay attention to the khuntkatti tenures, which is a local variant for bhuinhari. Nowhere in the Act was defined a criterion that was to be applied in determining lands of the tenants (bhuinhari) and that of landlords (manjhihas). The decisions were arbitrary and consequently unsatisfactory. Although this mistake was perpetuated when the Rent Act (Act I of 1879) was enacted. Moreover, in 1876, the *Chota Nagpur Encumbered Estates Act* (Act VI of 1876) was passed which empowered the Commissioner to appoint a Manager and to vest in him the entire management of encumbered estates.[6]

The *Chota Nagpur Landlord and Tenant Procedure Act* (Act I of 1879) tried to regulate the relations of landlords and tenants. Tenants of lands locally known as bhuinhari, khuntkatti and korkar were protected from enhancement, and a special procedure was laid down for the enhancement of rent of other occupancy raiyats (section 21). It continued restrictions on the sale of landed property, and it was accordingly declared that no under-tenure could be sold for arrears of rent without the consent of the Commissioner (section 123).[7]

Although these legislations failed to improve the conditions of the tribes of Chotanagpur. It has been established that during 1883-84 in the Chotanagpur division 447 land transactions took place in which 374 raiyats were affected. Again, during 1892-93, 1516 transactions/ mortgages of land took place in which 1289 raiyats suffered. Land sale also increased remarkably in Santhal Pargana. Although regulation III of 1872 recognised tenant rights and also guaranteed security of tenure and fixity of rent, it was of no avail to restrict interest to 24%. Within ten years of the settlement, 10,000 court sales and 40,000 private sales of raiyati holdings have been noted. The pace of the colonisation of the tribal regions can be judged from the incidence of immigration. In Chotanagpur alone, for instance, between 1871 and 1931, the immigrants rose from 96,000 to 307,000.[8] The agrarian discontent prevalent among the tribes of Chotanagpur manifested itself in the form of *Sardar Larai* or the *Mulkui Larai* (the struggle for land) movement in Ranchi district. Though the movement started earlier but it gained momentum after the failure of the Chotanagpur Tenures Act (1869). The agitation continued for four decades and constituted the background of the Birsa movement.[9]

THE SARDAR MOVEMENT:

The Sardar (the leader) meant the educated Christian Mundas who protested against the incidence of forced labour (beth-begari). The leaders of the Sardar movement were mainly Mundas, many of whom had received a primary education and were Christians. However many Oraons and non-Christian adivasis also took part in the movement. The Sardars (participants in the movement) thought as the original settlers of Ranchi district, the Adivasis had an inalienable right of free (or virtually free) use of all land in the district. The Sardars felt that the dikus had no right to make heavy impositions on them. Thus the Christian Mundas and Oraons better known as Sardars wanted to regain low-rent or rent-free lands that they had lost. They sometimes demanded in addition the right to govern their villages by themselves. They adopted means of 'prayer, petition and protest' to win back their freedom. They collected funds to fight legal battles for the restoration of their lost rights and land. They were not disloyal to the Crown, not even the Raja of Chotanagpur in the initial stages. Occasionally they turned out the rent collectors and did not pay rent, and sought forcible occupation of their ancestral lands, which the landlords had captured.[10]

Immediately after the mutiny of 1857, we find first instances of Sardar activity. In 1858-59 some Adivasis seized Diku land, and there were scuffles. In an attempt to reduce tension, the government between 1858 and 1862 reinstated a few hundred Adivasi families on traditional low-rent tenures in the south-eastern part of Ranchi district. The adivasis in this area were pacified. But agrarian unrest broke out anew in other adivasi areas in the middle 1860s, and in 1867 the Sardars submitted a petition seeking restoration of low-rent holdings.[11]

In the Munda society, and indeed among all tribals, the land usually classified as 'Khuntkatti' and 'Bhuinhari' belonged to the entire village. Now forged documents of lands were prepared and with the help of the rulers and courts, tribals began to be dispossessed of their land. In the beginning, the king or the British rulers used to collect a fixed revenue. Gradually the greedy thekedars and zamindars began to extort money from the tribal on different pretext. This is evident from the following excerpt drawn from a government record of 1869:

"If a horse was needed the Kol had to pay for it. If the zamindar needed a palki not only the Mundas and Oraons had to pay for it but had also to carry it. All expenses of the zamindar, like for their singers, the cows producing milk and betel leaves had to be borne by the tribals. If there was a death in the family of the zamindar entire expenses of the rituals had to be defrayed by

the tribals. It was also mandatory for the tribals to present gifts whenever a child was born in the zamindar's family. In case a thekedar was convicted in a court, the penalty had to be deposited by the Kol. Even in case of the birth of a child in a tribal family they were forced to give presents to the zamindars and thekedars. Apart from all these, the tribals had to work for the zamindars and thekedars as 'Begars' without receiving any payment."[12]

Another reason for the agrarian discontent was as the Settlement Officer pointed out in his report in 1903 that the privileged lands of the landlords (manjhihas) kept on increasing and the lands of Munda tenants prepared by them (bhuinhari) constantly decreasing by fraudulent means. The decrease in bhuinhari lands became the chief cause for the Sardar movement.[13] In about 1873, a Munda said to the senior Commissioner in charge of restoring adivasi lands:

"We claim bhuinhari rights because [Chota] Nagpur is our fatherland. We consider Nagpur as our Gaya, Ganga, Kasi and Prayag [sacred places in Hindu traditions]. The bones of our ancestors lie buried in the bowels of Nagpur...There exists in Sutiamba [20 miles north of Ranchi town] the ruins of our Munda fort...We allowed the Oraons... to come to this country. They came peaceably and we allowed them to occupy country in peace. I cannot say how or when the Hindus came to this country."[14]

The Sardars persuaded not only the ordinary members, but also the head or leaders of the village such as the munda (the civil head of a Munda village) or khunt pahan (the religious head) of the locality, to refuse all payment due to the superior landlord. Sardar leaders toured adivasi villages to raise money, gather signatures for their petitions and encourage adivasis to make claims to the visiting officials. The sardars sent memorials to the Commissioner, the Lieutenant-Governor General and the Secretary of State. They insisted on their right to the land and told how the foreign landlords had taken their property.

The following is an excerpt from a petition drawn by the sardars to the Commissioner of Chota Nagpur:

"We the Mundas of eight Parganas of Chotanagpore beg respectfully to lay before your Honour the following prayers, and hope you will be good enough to consider them duly. That the measurement of Bhooihurree lands in Chotanagpore made by the special Commissioner Babu Rakhal Dass and others is not rightly done. He measures the land which the Ticcadars say; they strike off the claim of the Mundas from their ancestral lands. Therefore we the Mundas do not at all agree with the measurement made by the Native Special Commissioners. They have put aside the claim of many from their ancestral land and the Ticcadars consequently began to oppress us excessively. And therefore the inhabitants fly to Assam to escape oppression, their lands being dispossessed by the Elakadar. If Chotanagpore does not belong to the Mundas, it belongs to none- neither to Ticcadars or Elakadars nor to the Nagbunsis. Chotanagpore was established by the Mundas and possessed by them."[15]

There were three phases through which the Sardar agitation evolved: the agrarian phase (1858-81), the revivalist phase (1881-90) and the political phase (1890-95). The substratum of the movement, however, remained agrarian.[16]

The widespread disturbances during 1858-59 marked the beginning of the agrarian phase. In October 1858, the Christians of the villages near Jhagara resisted their zamindar who oppressed them; in November 1858 at Bala there was a clash between a Jagirdar and his ryots. In September 1867, 14000 Christians filed a petition against local officers and the Raja of Chotanagpur. This along with other factors facilitated the passage of Act I of 1869 which provided for the restoration of bhuinhari lands to the ryots. The bhuinhari settlement marked the end of the disputes centring on bhuinhari and majhias tenures of lands, but its overall results fell short of the expectations of Sardars, who would be satisfied with nothing short of a restoration of all the lands of which they or their ancestors had ever held possession. Moreover, the operation was not extended to cover such tenures as rajhas, khuntkatti and korkar, which caused fresh troubles between zamindars eager to convert them into their personal cultivable possession and the resisting ryots. The petition dated 17 May 1876 submitted by the German mission complained against the native Commissioners, of whom the Mundas were suspicious, and called for the abolition of manifold imposts, taxes etc. The Government while sympathising with the benevolent motives that actuated the members of the mission in promoting the welfare of the Kols 'warned them' against entertaining any notion that the Kols would gain any secular advantages by embracing Christianity, and turned down the complaint against the native Commissioners.[17]

The agitation, however, continued and passed into a revivalist phase during the eighties. In a petition dated 25 March 1879, the Mundas claimed that Chotanagpur belonged to them. The result was foreseeable: the Government found the petitions to be "unreasonable" and "extravagant" and the appeals were rejected. Some of the Sardars reacted violently. They tried to get their co-tribals to see that they could never realize their hope for liberty unless they managed the country themselves. They proceeded to call both public and private meetings to rouse their courage, collect money, dissuade people from becoming Christian, forced them not to go to the churches and asked them to remove their children from the Mission schools. In 1881, a group of sardars tried to set up a Raj (kingdom) at Doesa, a former seat of the Raja of Chota Nagpur. The Sardars were quite strong in and around Lohardaga.[18]

From 1890 the Sardar movement turned against all Europeans, both missionaries and officials, who were suspected of acting hand in glove with the zamindars. The Mundas thought that all had turned against them, and that there was no alternative to fighting unaided their own battle for the recovery of their land. The constitutional methods had not yielded any results. A new group of people emerged, the neo-Sardars, who thought that the root cause of their malady was the British rule which protected their enemies; therefore it must be ended. In September 1892, these Sardars hatched a plot to kill all thekedars and German missionaries, but it misfired because they had no organization, no rallying point. They looked forward to the advent of a leader. Hoffmann observed:

"At that time I have heard Sardars say: We have appealed to the Sardar for redress and got nothing. We have turned to the missions, and they too have not saved us from the dikus. Now there is nothing left with us but to look to one of our own men."[19]

Therefore, the Sardar Larai started as a petition movement against landlords' beth-begari and encroachments on bhuinhari lands; the sardars demanded that they pay rent directly to the Government. Mohapatra argues that the

Sardar Larai was the first serious challenge to the concept of landlord property, which was at the basis of the Permanent Settlement. There were two levels at which the struggle took place. At the local agrarian and economic level within the village the revolt was led by either bhuinhars or Christian converts. At an overtly political level, it amounted to a struggle for the 'establishment of an alternative notion of power', 'the restoration of collective community property' and the 'negation of the landlord's claims of absolute property right.'[20] The movement was basically agrarian. The Sardars had first sought shelter in Christianity, then they broke away from the missions and turned to the Calcutta lawyers and finally clashed with the authorities.[21]

THE KHERWAR MOVEMENT

Another movement of the nineteenth century which had agrarian discontent as its root cause was the Kherwar movement of the Santal tribes in Chotanagpur. Most of the Santal tribes were landless agricultural labourers as they were evicted from their traditional landholdings. The changing forms of appropriation by the creditor were noticed during this phase of intensive colonialism. The problem was most acute in the tribal areas. For instance, the Santhals of Damin-e- Koh were reduced to a condition of serfdom in which they could not buy a bullock, a utensil, or even a grain of the produce of their own. Though the revised Civil Procedure Code of 1877 prohibited the attachment by creditors of the "implements of husbandry", the peasants could still be pressurized to sell their articles in order to pay the creditors.[22]

The Kherwar Movement of 1874 under Bhagirath Manjhi occurred in the year of great scarcity and famine. Bhagirath by then was already a known political leader as he had been imprisoned in 1868 for his participation in agrarian unrest and in 1871 for his agitation at the time of first census.[23] In his meetings he asserted that the land which they and their ancestors reclaimed and made cultivable belonged to them and that no government could demand taxes from them. He told the people that he was sent by God to redress their grievances, to fight for them, to mitigate their sufferings and to establish the Santal Raj which will be free from scarcity, tyranny and oppression. He ordered them to meet at Bowsee, the place where he was appointed as king. He received rent payments, and issued receipts to the people and asked them not to pay any dues to the government or the Zamindar.[24]

To suppress the movement, the government took strong action. The Deputy Commissioner Boxwell demolished the shrine set up at Taldiha (Godda), carried away the image and took the Santhal Pandit, Bhagirath and his brother to Dumka. They were sentenced to two years imprisonment.[25] An extra- detachment of troops from 4th Native Infantry from Bhagalpur was stationed at Dumka and new police posts were established. Ultimately, the troops were withdrawn in 1877 when the agitation was thought to have subsided. In Sultanabad district, another leader, Gyan Parganait, ordered the Santhals to cleanse themselves and stop paying rent to the government. For this, Gyan was sentenced to seven years of imprisonment.[26]

Bhagirath was released in 1877. Though he settled down to become a quiet and peaceful religious reformer, he continued his work in a secret way. It was discovered later that the movement did not die and there did exist a distinct organization of Kherwars which was silently spreading and strengthening it. Bhagirath died in 1879 but a new movement against the census operation was launched, and it was more violent than any other movement since the Santhal Revolt of 1855.[27]

The new disturbances had its seat in the Hazaribagh district of Chotanagpur. The new messiah Dubia Gosain had travelled through several districts of Chotanagpur and by austerities which he practiced succeeded in attracting the notice of the people. He had three Santhal agents, one of whom had been employed in the police. This movement was an outcry against the census operation of 1881 which was raised by the tribal peasants of Jamtara under the influence of Dubia Gosain. Their manifestations were confined to complaints and petitions containing long expostulations on local matters such as rates of rent, or the system of Chaukidari payment.

It was reported that some five men appeared before the sub-divisional magistrate of Dumka with some fragments of papers, which they said had fallen from heaven. They said that they had been directed by deity to take them to magistrate. The Dy. Commissioner of Santhal Pargana enquired into the matter and found out these men were aggrieved at the disappearance of the village grazing land under the operation of the settlement. Both the divisional officers of Dumka and Deoghar enquired into the matter and found out no other reason than the anger of the people caused by settlement operation. With due warning these men were discharged.[28]

In 1880-81, the Kherwars tried their best to revive a tribal administration. The sub-divisional officers of Dumka was besieged in his tent by a huge group of Santal agitators, shouting for the whole night. This was followed by the burning down of the sub-divisional headquarters at Jamtara. Cosserat, the Officer-in-charge of the Census for the Damin-i-koh, was surprised and taken prisoner at Katikhund. Objections were taken to the numbering of the houses and of the people to record their names, while the fact that the final enumeration was to be carried out at night lent colour to the apprehension that government meditated some widespread policy of violence. The census operation was mistaken for yet another occasion when fresh tax would be levied and/ or the Santals would be forced to become Christians and/or that their women would be branded and/or the men would be deported or sent to the Afghan war.[29]

Before the final enumeration, set for the night of the 17th February 1881, the whole Santal Parganas was in a state of unrest. The house of Jamtara magistrate was burned down, prisoners were freed from jail in Katikhund.[30] The Government feared a general uprising. In order to overawe the Santals, a body of military police was posted in the district and a field force of 4,500 cavalry and infantry was sent up under Colonel Gordon. Troops marched through the district, and these measures proved effective in preventing any further disturbance. In order not to provoke the Santals, the final enumeration was cancelled by the Governor-General.[31] In other districts with a Santal population, the final enumeration in Santal villages was made during the day instead of night.[32]

In order to suppress the influence of Dubia Gossain, the Government took punitive action and Dubia Gossain was taken prisoner and was deported to Lucknow, far away from the Santals as a political prisoner.[33] The other ring leaders were also arrested during and after the Census Operation and sentenced to imprisonment or deportation. The rumours as well as the rigid stand of the Santals against Census Operations 'reflected the community consciousness of the Santals bound by loyalty to their leaders and to their radical ideas...The new mood of solidarity created by the Kherwar movement had throughout a bitter anti-state tone. Its primary reason was the growing antipathy of Santals towards the government'. Though the Kherwar movement died down soon, but the radical faith in the creation of Santal Raj persisted.[34]

From a close scrutiny of the sources available on the Kherwar movement, it appears that it was mainly directed against the colonization of area. It was an agrarian issue and not religious one because the demands of Santals included the restoration of their land, opposition to enhancing rent and encroachment to their grazing land and forest wealth, although they made use of the religious myths, legends and superstitions for uniting the people to launch struggle for their economic betterment.[35]

In order to find out the nature of the Kherwar movement a series of twelve questions was sent to all the colonial authorities and the Zamindars of the areas. Almost all of them confirmed that the movement was widespread. Maharaja Gopal Chandra Singh of Maheshpur reported that the opposition to census did spread rapidly. Babu Taresh Nath Pande of Pakur reported that the Santals objected to the counting of houses taking place at night. Apart from actual opposition there were rumours everywhere near Hazaribagh. The Santals did not want the names of sister-in-law and brother-in-law to be registered together. They apprehended that the men were to be sent as coolies; in some war; some said that new poll tax was to be levied and that all able-bodied men was to be sent to Cachar to work in the tea plantation.

Some Santals said the government was going to recruit them in the army to be sent to Kabul in Afghan war. Babu Ram Kanai Karforma admitted that low classes of Hindus, the Bhuiyas, the Goalas, Kols, the Chamars, the Jolahas, the Doms, the Koeries and the Kurmies – all of them objected to the Census operation. Several excuses were made by the Santal but in the heart of their heart they believed that it was the intention of the government to enhance their rent. Even the colonial authorities at local level were convinced that imposition of rent and its enhancement were the real issues for their uneasiness. The Santals were aggrieved that the settlement had deprived them of all those privileges which they and their forefathers had enjoyed since long.[36]

CONFLICT OVER FOREST RIGHTS:

The concept of the 'Adivasi' and the 'Forest' is inseparable, although the word 'Adivasi' literally means original inhabitants whose economic organization and means of livelihood were based on forest ecology. The forests, since ancient times had been of crucial significance in the socio-economic life as well as ritual life of the adivasis. However, since the second half of the 19th century they were prohibited from unrestricted use of the forest.[37]

The advent of British rule introduced commercialization of agriculture with new sets of land settlements which intensified the process that evicted the adivasis from their own agricultural land and prevented their easy access to forest resources. Prior to the British annexation of Chotanagpur, tribals normally enjoyed customary access to all forest produce. They could also clear the forest for extension of cultivation with the increase of population and to graze their cattle. These practices were regulated by the *mundas* (headman of the village) and the *mankis* (*pir*). Nevertheless, neither the forest, nor the trees were considered to be the property of the indigenous kings or their subordinates.[38]

Till about the 1850s the British did not attempt to control and regulate forests; they were only interested in collecting some dues on timber export and grazing through the contract system. Increasing demand for timber, particularly for railway sleepers, instantly made the Sal forests of Chotanagpur valuable and provided impetus for extending control over them. There was also a growing demand for the timber of these forests in the timber marts of Calcutta where they were used for building purposes. A large quantity also went to the Sunder bans for boat building and dry poles were exported to the coal fields and to other parts of Bengal and Bihar. Thus while forests became increasingly restricted for the local people, they were commercialised on a massive scale in the interests of enabling sustained timber production.

The statement of the Deputy Commissioner of Santal Parganas reveals the changing attitude of the Government, when he said, "There was at that time no railways, no trade, no steam and there was all over the country far more forest than any one wanted...and the policy if the Government of the day was to clear (jungle) not to preserve...but things are changed as regards the forest. There are two railways running through the Santal Parganas...lines of steamers and fleets of boats on the river. The plains formerly covered with forest... are now cleared and densely populated...Now the policy of the Government in its own estates is to preserve and not to destroy."[39]

In the 1860s, the government made the first attempts to control Chotanagpur's forests and restrict the traditional access to the forests in the interests of preserving its timber. In September 1864, Dr. Anderson, the Superintendent of the Royal Botanical Garden, Calcutta, was appointed by the Bengal government to furnish his views about forest conservation. He reported the customary practices, such as tapping sal trees for 'dhoona' or resin and the system of cotton culture followed by the tribals as being destructive of the forests.[40] Although Dalton, the Commissioner of Chotanagpur Division, proposed to place forests under the charge of the mundas and mankis who were assigned the responsibility of protecting the forests.[41] This dependence on the traditional leaders was necessitated by the remoteness of Chotanagpur's forests from the major timber marts and the inability of the colonial government to provide for any other agency at the time.

Behind such initiatives was the colonial government's understanding that timber from the Chotanagpur forests would become commercially more valuable in the future when the forests near the timber marts were exhausted and when better communication were established with the interior. The commercial intent was, however, masked by public pronouncements of ecological concerns.[42] Dalton thus declared that 'it is not solely for the sake of timber that the forests should be preserved, it is desirable to afford them protection in consequence of the effect their disappearance is likely to have on the rainfall.'[43] Nevertheless, despite such considerations, extension of settled cultivation rather than reserving tracts of forests remained the focus of government policy in the mid nineteenth century. The revenue settlement of 1867 encouraged the reclamation of land for cultivation and Hayes, the Deputy Commissioner of Singhbhum, reported that thanks to the 'civilising' influence of the British, cultivation had increased and all wastelands near Chaibasa had disappeared.[44]

In 1871, Captain Losack, Deputy Conservator of Forests, made a rapid inspection of the Division. In 1873, W. Schlich, Conservator of Forests in Bengal, examined the Palamau forests. In 1875, the Saranda Pir forest in Singhbhum, covering an area of 400 square miles, was declared as Reserved Forest. In 1876, Koderma forest, covering an area of 60 square miles, was added to it.[45]

Moreover, the Indian Forest Acts of 1865 and 1878 were enacted by the Government for the management and preservation of forests. An attempt was made to regulate the collection of forest produce by the forest dwellers. Thus, the socially regulated practices of the local people were to be restrained by law. On the basis of the Government of India's forest policy issued on 19 October 1894, India's forests were divided into four groups: reserved forests, protected forests, private forests and village forests and wastes. While in the two latter groups the access for the village communities continued much as before, in the protected forests, the right of the local peasants to graze their animals, to cultivate crops, to fell trees, to collect honey, mahua, kusum leaves and sabai grass came under the strict control of the colonial state. The Forest department undertook the management of reserved and protected forests, while village forests were administered by district administration. The village headmen were assigned the responsibility of managing the village forests under the Deputy Commissioner.

The policy of reservation and protection of forests by the government interfered with the customary freedom to reclaim forest land and appropriate natural resources. Instead, tribals were allowed to collect essential supply of fire wood, thatching grass, fodder, date-palm, sal and leaves of other trees, bamboo and other forest produce for their domestic use from the reserved forest only on payment of an annual rate of two pice per rupee of land rent payable by them. Right to pasturage was restricted only to cattle – sheep and goats being excluded. Shifting cultivation was gradually abandoned.

To justify the intrusion of colonial forest administration, the government argued that forest laws were designed to secure the best interest of the tribals. The government depicted the tribals as destroyers of their habitat. A district gazetteer for instance commented, 'Unfortunately, the Kol seems unable to grasp the fact that the forest was made for any purpose other than to be destroyed, and its timber wasted wholesale.'[46]

It was argued that all the villages outside the protected forests would soon be denuded of vegetation, unless immediate preventive measures were taken. It was also stated that the right of the tribals were merely suspended in their own interests and not completely taken away. Forests had to be protected 'for the interests of the tenants, both of the present and future generations – and in view of this consideration it is equitable to curtail the privileges of the present generation of tenants, provided that no excessive inconvenience is caused to them.'[47] The object of restricting access to the forests was ostensibly not to exclude or diminish the rights of the tenants, but to regulate the exercise of their rights and prevent their wanton abuse.

Thus, traditional forest activities, not being conducted for earning profit, were termed wasteful, while destruction of large areas of forests for the sake of the timber trade was a commercially profitable venture and hence denoted a gainful utilisation of forest resources. Tribal communities of Chotanagpur had to face a new kind of alienation. In place of open access to the forests there now appeared fences and forest guards. In place of rights there emerged privileges and offences. In place of customary use based on local need, there emerged a set of restrictions.

People protested against the curtailment of their customs and the restraints imposed by the rules of the Forest Department in different ways. There were both individual and organised acts of defiance, which were reported on a large scale in successive forest departmental reports, as well as attempts at constitutional protest through debates on forest issues at the provincial legislative assembly initiated by tribal members. Rather than large-scale protest movements, in the normal course of affairs, the grievances of the people were translated into a silent disregard of forest rules. Disregard of forest rules was common in Chotanagpur and Santhal Parganas. For unauthorised felling of trees and grazing cattle, people were almost regularly fined.

Table 5.3: Forest crimes in the reserved and protected forests of, 1911-12 to 1931-32

	Singhbhum		Chaibasa/Kolhan	
Year	Felling	Grazing	Felling	Grazing
1911/12	108	12	32	19
1912/13	33	5	05	28
1913/14	30	2	04	24
1914/15	77	5	14	34
1915/16	49	1	36	31
1916/17	19	2	83	12
1917/18	98	2	97	4
1918/19	97	2	52	2
1919/20	86	3	21	3
1920/21	42	6	35	-
1921/22	94	1	51	1
1922/23	66	6	92	11
1923/24	70	8	77	14
1924/25	69	8	64	17
1925/26	54	7	68	13
1926/27	30	-	70	11
1927/28	82	2	77	1
1928/29	75	6	21	2
1929/30	116	5	25	-
1930/31	92	7	82	6
1931/32	104	1	89	6

Source: Annual Progress Report on Forest Administration in the Province of Bihar and Orissa', 1911-12 to 1931-32.

Every year, the Forest Department reported a number of cases involving arson, poaching, illegal removal of firewood, illegal grazing, avoidance of begar and non-payment of wood cess and other forest cess. The frequency of such occurrences varied from time to time. The famine conditions of 1913-18, for instance, resulted in a spurt of such 'offences'. Owing to failure of the rice crop in 1918, thousands of people supplemented their scanty food supply with edible fruit, roots, leaves and flowers. The scarcity forced the Deputy Commissioner to open parts of the forest, which resulted in an increase in offences such as poaching and felling.

The struggle over forests was a significant aspect of the Non-Cooperation movement in Chotanagpur as well. Many Kherwars participated in this movement demanding the restoration of the customary rights of tribals to extract timber and collect forest produce for their own consumption. In fact, Swaraj meant to them the restoration of their right to the forests. Tribals began to cut down the jungles on the grounds that only they were entitled to these jungles. There were cases of 'illicit cutting' in the government reserved forests. The hill side jungle in Ranka was cleared for jhum cultivation.[48]

The Congress also organized a series of forest Satyagraha demanding the tribal customary right to use timber, roots, fruits, honey etc. for their livelihood. 'Forest Satyagraha' — the reassertion by poor peasants and tribals of traditional customary rights over forests 'reserved' by the colonial state – represents an almost forgotten but fascinating aspect of Gandhian era.[49] A batch of ten Ho volunteers under the leadership of Harihar Mahto violated the forest act on 6th August 1930 by cutting down about hundred Sal trees in Lepungbera forest at the distance of about seven miles from Chakradharpur. Soon the situation became alarming in the district and to curtail it the administration swung into action. Harihar Mahto was arrested and imprisoned. A congress worker Hari Singh was also arrested in connection with forest Satyagraha. He was imprisoned for one year and fined rupees twenty. Another forest Satyagraha was organized among the Kharwars of Palamau under the leadership of Jadubans Sahay and some other Congress leaders.[50]

There were also attempts to pressurise the government regarding the hardships of the people through parliamentary means. In his speech of 14 February 1924 at the Bihar and Orissa Legislative Council Dulu Manki, the Member for Singhbhum Non-Mohammedan Rural Constituency, articulated the grievances of the people by pointing out that at the time of declaring the jungle as 'reserved forest', the people of the villages adjacent to the forest were given the assurance that they would be allowed to take home fuel, leaves and timber and graze their cattle there. However, in practice, they invariably found that they were not allowed to do so. Articles which a cultivator required were not given to them without a fee. Nor were they allowed to take forest products that were essential for their livelihood.[51]

Dulu Manki's resolution, which had been passed in the Legislative Assembly, recommended to the Government that, people be permitted to take fuel, sabai grass and home materials free of charge from the protected forests.[52]

In this way, the colonial forest policy with its commercial pre-occupations resulted in a series of deprivations which not only made the tribals economically weaker and subject to various forms of exploitation, but also forced them to abandon their customary religious taboos. Their entire relationship to the forest was thus altered in a growing estrangement from what had been their exclusive environment and had now turned into a preserve of superior outsider interests.[53]

NOTES AND REFERENCES

1.   Shukla, P.K. "Tribal Resistance in Chotanagpur: A Case Study of the Dubia Gossain Movement (1870-80)." *Proceedings of the Indian History Congress*, vol. 62, 2001, pp. 613-20.

2.   Peter Tete, S.J. *A Missionary Social Worker in India: J.B. Hoffmann, the Chota Nagpur Tenancy Act and the Catholic Cooperatives 1893-1928*, Roma, 1984, p. 16.

3.   Sinha, B.B. *Socio-Economic Life in Chotanagpur*, Delhi, 1979, p. 9.

4.   Reid, J. *Final Report on the Survey and Settlement Operations in the District of Ranchi 1902-1910*, Calcutta, 1912, p. 35.

5.   Peter Tete, S.J. op cit. pp.15-16.

6.   Reid, J. op cit. pp.35-36.

7.   Ibid, p. 37.

8.   Shukla, P.K. op. cit. pp. 613-20.

9.   Chattoraj, A.K. 'Mulkui Larai in Chotanagpur: Genesis and Impact" in Asha Mishra, C.K. Paty (ed.) *Tribal Movements in Jharkhand 1857-2007*, New Delhi, 2009, p. 94.

10. MacDougall, John. "Agrarian reform vs. Religious revitalization: Collective Resistance to Peasantization among the Mundas, Oraons, and Santals, 1858-95", *Contributions to Indian Sociology*, vol. 11, no.2 (1977), pp. 295-321.

11. De Sa, Fidelis. *Crisis in Chotanagpur*, Redenptorist Publications: Bangalore, 1975, pp.93-94. See also MacDougall, John. op. cit. pp.302-303.

12. Cited in Dhan, A.K. *Birsa Munda,* Publication Division: New Delhi, (kindle edition), p.202.

13. Meena, K.P. Adivasi Vidroh, Anugya Books: Delhi, 2021, pp. 87-88.

14. Unpublished government report quoted in MacDougall, John. op. cit. p.305.

15. The Mundas to the Commissioner of Chota Nagpur, Ranchi, March 25, 1879, cited by S.C. Roy, *The Mundas and their Country*, Calcutta, 1912, p.282.

16. Singh, K.S. *Birsa Munda and His Movement 1874-1901: A study of a Millenarian Movement in Chotanagpur*, Oxford University Press: Calcutta, 1983, p.33.

17. Ibid, pp.33-35.

18. Peter Tete, S.J. op cit. p.19.

19. J.B. Hoffman to A. Forbes, 14 January 1900 quoted in Singh, op. cit. p.35.

20. Mohapatra, P.P. "Class Conflict and Agrarian Regimes in Chota Nagpur, 1860-1950", *The Indian Economic and Social History Review*, vol. 28:1, 1991, p.36.

21. Singh, K.S. op. cit. p.197.

22. Shukla, P.K. op. cit. pp. 613-14.

23. Anderson P.B. "Revival, Syncretism and the Anticolonial Discourse of the Kherwar Movement, 1871-1910", in Young, R.F. (ed.) *India and the Indianness of Christianity*, Eerdmans Publishing Co., U.S.A, 2009, p.136.

24. Jha, A.P. "Nature of the Santhal Unrest of 1871-1875 and Origin of the Sapha Hor Movement", *Indian Historical Records Commission* (Proceedings) 35, pt. 2 (1960), pp. 103-113.

25. Anderson P.B. op. cit. p. 137.

26. Sinha, S.P. *Conflict and Tension in Tribal Society*, Concept Publishing Company: New Delhi, 1993, p.202.

27. Shukla, P.K. op. cit. pp. 615-16.

28. Ibid p. 616.

29. Hodne, Olav. *"L.O. Skrefsrud, Missionary and Social Reformer among the Santals of Santal Parganas: With Special Reference to the Periods between 1867 and 1881"*, Oslo, 1966, p. 272.

30. O'Malley, L.S.S. *Bengal District Gazetteers: Santal Parganas*, Calcutta, 1910, p.59.

31. Letter dated 8th June 1881, from G.N. Barlow, Commissioner, Bhagalpur and Santal Parganas to the Secretary, Judicial Department, Government of Bengal.

32. Sinha, S.P. op. cit. pp. 207-208.

33. "Santal Disturbances", *The Englishman*, 22nd Feb. 1881.

34. Sinha, S.P. op. cit. p. 210.

35. Shukla, P.K. op. cit. p.619.

36. Ibid.

37. Mallick Ata. *Encroachment on the Rights of the Adivasis: Colonial Forest Policy in 19th century Chotanagpur and Santal Parganas. Proceedings of the Indian History*

Congress, vol. 73, Indian History Congress, 2012, pp. 747-55.

38. Gupta, S.D. "Accessing Nature: Agrarian Change, Forest Laws and their Impact on an Adivasi Economy in Colonial India", *Conservation and Society*, 7(4), 2009, pp. 227-238.

39. Letter from the Deputy Commissioner of Santhal Parganas to the Commissioner of Bhagalpur division and Santhal Parganas, dated 28th January 1893, Government of Bengal, Revenue (Forest) Proceedings, No. 7, February 1893.

40. Sinha, B.B. Socio- Economic Life in Chotanagpur 1858-1935, B.R. Publishing: Delhi, 1979, p.136.

41. Dalton to Board of Revenue, 3 August 1867, Government of Bengal, Revenue Proceedings, No.9, September 1867.

42. Gupta, S.D. op. cit. p.230.

43. Dalton to Board of Revenue, 3 August 1867, Government of Bengal, Revenue Proceedings, No.9, September 1867.

44. W.H. Hayes to Commissioner, Chota Nagpur Division, 22 February 1867, p. 128, Government of Bengal, Revenue Proceedings, No. 122, June 1867.

45. Sinha, B.B. op. cit. pp.137-138.

46. O' Malley, L.S.S. *Bengal District Gazetteers: Singhbhum, Seraikela and Kharsawan*, The Bengal Secretariat Book Depot: Kolkata, 1910, p.102.

47. Hallett, Deputy Commissioner, Singhbhum to the Commissioner of Chotanagpur Division, 26 July 1916, Government of Bihar and Orissa, Revenue (Forest)

Proceedings, No. 4, A- Enclosure (1), April 1917, Bihar State Archives.

48. Singh, Lata. *Popular Translations of Nationalism Bihar, 1920-1922*, New Delhi, 2012, pp.192-193.

49. Sarkar, Sumit. "Primitive Rebellion and Modern Nationalism: A Note on Forest Satyagraha in the Non-Cooperation and Civil Disobedience Movements", *Proceedings of the Indian History Congress*, vol. 38 (1977), pp. 511-523.

50. Rana, L.N. "Politics in Jharkhand during the Civil Disobedience Movement (1930-1934)", *Proceedings of the Indian History Congress*, vol. 66 (2005-2006), pp. 1101-1118.

51. Gupta, S.D. *Adivasis and the Raj: Socio- Economic Transition of the Hos 1820-1932*, Orient Blackswan, New Delhi, 2011, pp. 198-199.

52. Resolution of Legislative Council, Government of Bihar and Orissa, Revenue (Forest) Proceedings, No. 18A, Encl. 1, October 1924.

53. Gupta, S.D. (2011) pp.200.

CHAPTER III
MILLENARIAN MOVEMENTS

The Santhal, Munda and Ho movements believed in the supernatural intervention and reposed faith in their rebel leaders as redeemers. This belief is termed as millenarianism. The movements illustrate two crucial elements of millenarianism: appearance of a charismatic leader as the exponent of its radical ideology, and the pervasive belief among the rebels that their cause would inevitably triumph because it has been blessed by a supernatural agency.[1]

Millenarian movements were not always spontaneous, but were quite organized, coordinated and prudent. Their conviction was firm that they would definitely be victorious. This conviction was inspired by a religious faith in a supernatural intervention, and because of the involvement of the charismatic leader, these movements are also known as the 'messianic movements.'[2]

Another concept in connection with such movements is that of religious revitalization and cultural purification. The aim of these movements was either a complete religious reformation or a renaissance and a restoration of the old religious beliefs. The influence of Christian missionaries and western education and also the influence of Hindu religious ideology of the Dikus made the Adivasis rethink about their religious perception. We may observe elements of Christianity or Hinduism in the neo-tribal religion that emerged during this period. For example, monotheism, influence of gurus, wearing sacred thread, giving up meat and traditional liquor, cleanliness, and abandonment of witchcraft – all were the outcome of Hindu influence.

Causes behind the Millenarian Movements

The arrival of Christian missionaries in Chotanagpur was an event of great importance in the history of Chotanagpur. The main Missions which worked in Chotanagpur are the Anglican mission (1842, Hazaribagh), the Gossner Evangelical Lutheran (GEL) mission (1845, Ranchi), the Santal Mission of the Northern Churches (1866), the Church Missionary Society (1868), the Catholic Mission (1869), the Santal Mission of the United Free Church of Scotland (1869), the Fellowship of Christian Assemblies Mission (1880), the Methodist Church (1884), the Dublin University Mission (1892), the Seventh Day Adventist Mission (1898), the British Churches of Christ's Mission (1909) and the Assembly of God (1927).[3]

Among these missionary groups, it was the GEL mission and the Catholic Mission which were able to make a powerful, positive impression of Christianity among the tribals by offering them liberation from oppression by the landlords who were perceived to be hand in glove with the colonial rulers. Receiving baptism was seen as a means to obtain agrarian security and social protection. Thousands of tribals sought baptism and this inaugurated a mass movement.[4]

The mass movement in Jharkhand picked up momentum in late 1880s after the arrival of a zealous, hardworking, ingenious Jesuit missionary, Father Constant Lievens in Chotanagpur. Already by 1885, there were eight stations in

Chotanagpur run by the Belgian Catholic missionaries.[5] He championed the cause of the aboriginals against the landlords and moneylenders, helping the oppressed win their cases at court. He learned the Munda system, their traditional rights and claims which were sanctioned by their laws and customs. He made up his mind to help them, but at the same time to be prudent so as not to antagonize the Government.[6] Gradually, there began a 'mass movement' from the aborigines, seeking baptism.

Another great missionary of Chotanagpur was Father Hoffmann, who began his missionary life in the Munda country of Sarwada, which made him keenly aware of the grave problems of injustice by the Diku landlords, the lease holders and the moneylenders. And he rendered the greatest service to Chotanagpur through his extraordinary knowledge of the language and customs of Mundas. His 16 volumes of 'Encyclopedia Mundarika' (1924-1938) encompassing in its pages the whole culture and civilization of the Munda people. Besides, it goes to the credit of Father Hoffmann that in December 1909, *Chota Nagpur Catholic Cooperative Credit Society* had started, which forwarded loans to the Adivasis in order to improve the economic conditions of the tribals and to free them from the clutches of moneylenders.[7]

Hundreds of schools were established thanks to the leadership of Father Van Hoeck, who was the Director of Schools in the Chotanagpur Mission of the Jesuits. Along with the Jesuits, several religious societies of Women (sisters/ nuns) came to work in Jharkhand. Some of the earlier ones were the Loreto Sisters (1890), Daughters of St. Ann, which was founded in Ranchi (1897), Order of the Sisters of St. Usruline (1903), etc.[8]

The advent of Christian missionaries in Jharkhand in the 19th century opened up the inaccessible hilly region to the dynamics of cultural change setting the motion of new consciousness. The Christian missionaries of different denominations made tremendous progress in Chotanagpur. The number of Catholic converts alone rose from 15,000 in 1887 to 71,270 in 1900.[9] The number of Christian converts continued to rise progressively in Chotanagpur affecting the social and political life in the region and exposing the converts to the outside influence. There was no other region of tribal middle India which witnessed such a spread of Christianity. As Christianity spread it performed many roles: it gave the tribes a sense of identity; it gave them a history and a myth; it accentuated the notion of private rights in land; it promoted education and medical care; it also emphasized among the converts a sense of separateness from the rest.[10]

The second half of the nineteenth century witnessed the increased social, educational and philanthropic activities of the *Brahmo Samaj* in the region. Charitable homeopathic dispensaries, Mandirs, clubs and libraries were established at different places and educational activities were pursued. The Samaj waged war against the Hindu caste system, purdah system and child marriage and favoured the re-marriage of young Hindu widows. Hazaribagh was an important centre of Brahmoism from where, Brahmoism spread to many towns of Chotanagpur more prominently to Ranchi (1868) and Giridih (1874).[11]

The *Arya Samaj* arrived in Chotanagpur in the last decade of the nineteenth century and established its branch at Ranchi in 1894. It started publishing its weekly *Aryavarta* for dissemination of its ideology and programme and opened a school named 'Ved Vidyalaya' in 1900. Protection of women and girls against abduction and upbringing of orphans formed part of its active programme.[12] The *Ramakrishna Mission* opened its branch at Ranchi in 1917. It has to its credit many humanitarian and educational activities in different parts of the region. The idea of theism and neo-Vedanta of Swami Vivekananda influenced the Adivasis. The reforming sect of Vaishnavism also influenced the Adivasis of Chotanagpur. *Kabir Panthis* too converted the Munda and Oraons. The Hindu impact on the Adivasis led the 'God Shiva' becoming 'Mahadeo Bonga' and the 'Goddess Parvati' becoming 'Chandi Bonga'. The Adivasis adopted Dasai (Dashahara), Jitia, Mahadeo Manda Mela and other festivals.[13]

The genesis of any revitalization movement lays in the helplessness of a community to meet the onslaught of the machinery of oppression. Under severe 'ecological and politico-economic stress associated especially with colonial conquests and intense class exploitation, beliefs and rituals tends to be concerned with achieving a drastic improvement in the immediate condition of life and/or in the prospect of afterlife.' Their goal was restoration of egalitarian society. Wallace defines such movements as "deliberate, organized and conscious efforts by the members of a society to construct a more satisfactory culture."[14]

The advent of the Hindus and the Muhammadans had, no doubt, brought about perceptible changes in tribal socio-religious life, but their miseries, and esp. economic deprivation had also increased. Thus, after 1857, many tribals had embraced Christianity if not for salvation in next life, at least for economic benefits in this life. Land alienation was their greatest problem, but even Christianity failed to solve it. This was followed by the protracted Sardar Movement also known as Mulki Larai. This movement was led by the Christian ryots who showed that they could fight the zamindars. On the other hand, it also laid the foundation for the Birsa Movement as the Missionaries failed in getting restored to the ryots their alienated land. Administrative apathy, social discrimination and economic deprivation compelled the tribals to look for socio-religious regeneration and thus began the two great revivalist movements of the post-Company era, namely, the Sapha Hor movement and the Ulgulan Movement.[15]

SAPHA HOR MOVEMENT

The Sapha Hor movement was a puritan movement that originated among the Santhals in 1874 under the leadership of Bhagirath Manjhi of the village Tardiha in the Godda subdivision. He had also taken part in the Santhal rebellion led by Sidhu and Kanhu in 1855.[16] He had been imprisoned in 1868 for seditious conduct in trying to disturb people's mind by threatening an outbreak.[17]This movement aimed at reviving the golden age of the tribe when the Kherwar (the ancient name of the tribe) lived in idyllic happiness in legendary Champa to which their subsequent history was anti-climax. The dormant memory of God is awakened when anything extraordinary happens, a famine or epidemic, for instance. Then the Santhals feel guilty of abandoning their supreme God and worshipping the spirit, and they vow to reform themselves. This also explains the spasmodic character of the movement. In times of comparative plenty and prosperity very little is heard of it, during times of distress the movement revives.[18]

In 1871 Bhagirath Manjhi, the pioneer of the movement, started his mission as a religious teacher. He asked his follower to avoid all evil acts otherwise they would not get God's blessings. He asked them to narrate their actions to him. After hearing them, he used to admonish them for their wrong acts. He asked them to observe certain precepts, which in their essence were like the ten commandments of Christ. Stephen Fuchs, therefore believes that either he had been a Christian for some time or at any rate he was educated in a Christian school.[19]

Although Bhagirath was in favour of following the traditional religion he also advocated the worship of 'Singhbahini' i.e. Durga, the goddess of the Hindu zamindars. Sun, the traditional God of the Santals, was relegated to a second position. Besides these two, other Gods and Goddesses were not to be worshipped. A shrine of Singhbahini was erected at Tardiha, the birth place of Bhagirath, on Hindu pattern. At this shrine the worship of the deity was performed daily by a Santal priest. Sugar, sweets, meat, goat and a pair of pigeon were offered at the shrine.[20]

On every morning, Bhagirath's followers offered him a leaf-cup full of rice milk, a piece of betel nut and one pice. He advised his followers to kill all unclean animals – pigs and fowls – and abstain from drinking and dancing. By advocating the observance of a moral code, Bhagirath wanted them to become 'sapha hors' i.e. purists.

During the famine of 1874, Burma rice was imported. Bhagirath told his followers that they could see how God was working for them. The Sahibs i.e. the British were afraid. The rice which they brought was rice formerly given by the Santals to the bongas, and now brought back under some pretext.[21] He also declared that he was commissioned by the God to fight for the redressal of their grievances. He exhorted his followers to revolt at an opportune moment and advised them to wait till he gave them a signal to drive out all non-Kherwars from their area. But before he could give the required signal he was arrested. Deprived of their leaders the rebels did not have the courage to organize a revolt.[22]

Subsequently the movement launched by Bhagirath split into following three sects:

1. Purists (Sapha hors) worshipping Singhbahini and the Sun and totally abstaining from drinking and dancing.

2. Mendicants (babajis) whose profession was to traverse the country and beg

3. Half-hearted (bhelwargars), who while joining in all observances of the other Kherwars, retained their old customs also but substituted sweetmeats for animals in sacrificing.[23]

Dubu Gosain, a Hindu of Jagesar, was most among the mendicants. He claimed to possess supernatural powers. Like Sidhu and Kanhu, who circulated papers supposed to have been given to them by God, letters written on small scraps of paper were passed from village to village containing an order from Dubu Gosain to come to him immediately and practice the usages and customs of the Hindus. He also advised the Kherwars to stop worshipping their ancient deities. In this manner, Dubu Gosain tried to attract Santals towards Hinduism.

He also believed in the ideology of eschatolism i.e. the expectations of a world renewal through world- wide catastrophic upheavals. He, therefore, predicted several

calamities for those who disobeyed him. In 1880, he predicted
the occurrence of a deluge of fire-rain on the forthcoming
Dussehra which would destroy all those who persisted
in keeping unclean animals. On that day the 'raj' would be
handed over to him and his followers. Under them there
would be no oppression.[24]

As the prediction of a deluge was based on an old tradition
of the Kherwars, it was widely accepted by them. The non-
occurrence of the event forced Dubu to fix another date for
the dawn of millennium in which fields would yield fruits
without involving the labour of ploughing them and plenty
would flow to those who killed their fowls and pigs. In 1880-
81, Santal followers of Dubia Gosain circulated the following
statement:

"Receive the blessings of Dubia...Do not milk your cow or
plow your field on Sunday, neither keep or rear pigs or fowls.
Walk on the right path. Whoever comes to pay his respects to
me, all his desires shall be accomplished, but if my commands
are not obeyed as above stated, punishment will follow within
two or four months. My letters have already been sent to all
parts of the country. Make every person acquainted that his
welfare depends upon my blessings, and that...Bhagwan will
give whatever may be good for him...Whoever receives this
letter will make a fresh copy and circulate it; failing this he
will be held as guilty as of the sin of killing a cow."[25]

Undoubtedly the Sapha Hor movement had its root in
agrarian unrest and which had already been discussed at length
in the preceding chapter, their means were either religious
or devotional. Influence of Hinduism and Christianity
were clearly visible on the preaching of Bhagirath and the
subsequent mendicants. Among them Dubu Gosain was

more inclined towards Hinduism. By advising their followers to lead a pure life (life of a Sapha Hor) these mendicants tried to reform the tribal society. Bhagirath and other mendicants claimed to have been inspired by God to restore the golden age of their tribe. They believed in the ideologies of eschatology and millenarianism.

Although it is difficult to establish direct links between the Sapha Hor movement and Birsa's Ulgulan movement, a few similarities between the two are striking. Dubu Gosain's instructions to kill pigs and fowls and the prediction of a fire-rain, which did not come off, and Birsa thinking on these ideas were more or less similar. The emphasis on cleanliness and memory of the deluge by Birsa Munda might have been influenced by Dubu Gosain's views on them.[26]

BIRSA'S ULGULAN MOVEMENT

The Birsaite Ulgulan (Ulgulan means revolution in Mundari language) though built on the foundations established by Sardar Larai, buy there was no linear path connecting the latter to the former. The Christian missionaries played the catalytic role.

Birsa Munda was born on November 15, 1875 at Gareria Ulihatu village of P.S. Tamar.[27] His father Sugna, a poor peasant, was not able to maintain his children. As a child Birsa was adopted by his maternal aunt. He was employed on tending sheep and goats. As the lady did not treat him properly he fled to his eldest brother Konta who was at Bartoli. At Bartoli, Birsa met a German priest who took him to Barjo from where Birsa passed the Lower Primary Examination. In 1886, he shifted to Chaibasa from where he passed the Upper Primary

Examination in 1890. His parents had by then settled down in Chalkad and he decided to go there.[28]

Birsa was a bhuinhar, whose family had converted to Lutheranism a generation earlier. Birsa's father Sugna was a Lutheran catechist, and it was not surprising that young Birsa, like many others who grew up in the forest highlands of Arki and Bandgaon, attended the German mission school in Chaibasa between 1886 and 1890. Apparently, Birsa was present when Dr. Alfred Notrott, the Chaibasa mission-in-charge, delivered a 'sermon...on the theme of the Kingdom of Heaven', assuring his students 'that if they remained Christians and followed his instructions, he could get back all lands they had lost'. But with the growing disaffection between Munda Sardars and the Lutheran missionaries, Birsa increasingly heard the Sardars being called 'cheats'. He criticized Dr. Notrott and the missionaries in trenchant terms and so he was expelled from school in 1890 Birsa exclaimed 'sahib, sahib ek topi hai' (all whites, the British and the missionaries wear the same cap). Birsa and his family gave up their membership of the German mission in line with the Sardars' movement against it.[29]

For the next three years, Birsa worked in the house of Anand Panre, a Brahmin resident of Gaurbera, under whom he adopted Vaishnavite habits, including wearing of sacred thread and a sandalwood mark on the forehead, vegetarianism, and the worship of the tulsi plant. Thereafter, increasingly drawn into political activism during the final stages of the Sardar Larai, he left Gaurbera and wandered from place to place in search of food, work and a sense of purpose in life.[30]

Birsa first entered the colonial records in September 1895, when he was arrested for preaching radical ideas that alarmed government officials. He had started telling his friends that year that he had received the Divine word after a flash of lightning had struck him in the jungle.[31] At that time a smallpox epidemic broke out, villagers complained that Birsa's upstart ways had caused it and he was compelled to leave Chalkad only to return later once it was shown that the epidemic had continued to wreak havoc in his absence. Birsa's parents were also afflicted with the ailment. He returned home and nursed day and night not only them but also others who had been infected. His selfless service during the epidemic endeared him to all and he became an object of praise and adoration. People now believed that even his touch was magical and he possessed some divine power. Thus, the number of his followers multiplied instantly and people came from far-off places to listen to his discourses.[32]

Birsa claimed to be the Father of the Earth, *Dharti Aba*. He launched a bitter attack on the bongas, the priesthood of Bhagats, the authority of Pahan etc. A strict code of conduct was laid sown: theft, lying and murder were anathema: begging was prohibited. Slowly, he began to be identified as God himself. He was looked upon as an incarnation of Khasra Kora who had destroyed the Asurs.[33]

The purity of Munda religion was nearest to his heart and he constantly made attempts to remove all outside influences. With this object in mind, he propagated a new religion. Birsa's new religion was monotheist. The core of this religion was the worship of 'Singbonga'. The worship of any other spirit or deity was forbidden. It was mandatory to be non-vegetarian in Birsa's religion. The intoxicating drink 'haria', made of rice, and popular in Adivasi society was also discarded by the followers of Birsa's religion.[34]

The Christian missionaries informed the Government that Birsa was planning a conspiracy against the government and missionaries. He held night meetings in the hills and forests, and gradually drew over to his side not only the Mundas, but also the Oraons of the whole Chota Nagpur division. He promised his tribals that they will be unhurt in battle, since he would change English arms into water. Birsa had planned to begin his assault from Sarwada. Hoffmann and Rev. Lusty of the Anglican mission had reported about it to the authorities in Ranchi.[35]

Accordingly, the colonial government decided to keep vigilance on him but the constable who had been deputed to keep an eye on him was driven away from Chalkad.[36]W.H. Grimley, the Commissioner of Chotanagpur decided to arrest Birsa as he saw him as a 'fanatic' with 'preposterous ideas' and a disturber of public peace. On 22 August 1895, Police Superintendent G.R.K. Meares was entrusted with the responsibility of arresting Birsa under Section 353 and 505 of Indian Penal Code. This officer along with 20 sepoys, Rev. Lusty of Murhu Anglican Mission and Babu Jagmohan Singh Zamindar of Bandgaon arrested Birsa and his companions from his hut on 26 August 1895.[37]Birsa and his 15 principal followers were sentenced to 2 years' rigorous imprisonment. A fine of Rs. 50 was also imposed on Birsa, and in case of his failure to pay the same, his jail term was to be extended by another 6 months.

The second phase of Birsa movement began in 1897 when Birsa and his 15 followers were released from the Hazaribagh jail on the occasion of the Diamond Jubilee of Queen Victoria's reign. Birsa held night meetings which had a politico-religious slant. He reminded the people of the golden age (Satyuga) of their ancestors, of their need to resuscitate their ancient manners and religious customs and to regain their rights and property. In short, the Birsaites wanted to aim at establishing the Birsa religion and a Munda kingdom. They started visiting the temples and ancestral places beginning with Chutia, Jagannathpur, Nagpheni and New Rattan.[38]

Immediately after release, Birsa began organizing his followers. Dombari became the centre of Birsa's activities. Representatives of different areas assembled at Dombari in February 1898. The famine and epidemic of 1898 gave his followers an opportunity to render social service and enlist political support. Gradually, he collected a large body of archers and swordsmen and preached insurrection openly. A close associate Gaya Munda became the Chief of this force and Birsa's chief advisor. Panlu Munda, Johan Munda, Rirho Munda, Dukhan, Swansi Hathi Ram Munda, Domka Munda and Thipar Munda were the chief leaders of the movement. Members of Birsa Sena were stationed at Khunti, Ranchi, Chakradharpur, Bundu, Tamar, Karra, Torpa, Basia, Sisai etc.

The insurrection broke out as scheduled on Christmas Eve of 1899. The Christians had gathered in the church of Sarwada. The followers of Birsa visited the church, pretending to have come to listen to the carols, and shot arrows over and at the Christians. Fr. Hoffmann has written about the attack on himself and on his associate Fr. Carbery. The rebels even attacked the police stations. In the disturbance which broke out in Etkedih two constables lost their lives. The Khunti Police station was subjected to an attack during which one of the constables was savagely slashed by the mob.

On December 29,1899, H.C. Streatfield, the Deputy Commissioner of Ranchi, accompanied by Captain Roche and a body of troops, went to the scene of outrages and planned the arrest of Birsa. By January 9, 1900, it was established that Birsaites had hid themselves on Sail Rakab hill near Dombari because it had a defensive advantages with numerous caves inaccessible from all sides but one. They were armed with local weapons: bows and arrows, axes and slings etc. The police circled the hill. Firing followed which killed 300 men, women and children.[39]

After Sail Rakab, the movement fizzled out. Mundas were arrested on slightest suspicion. Houses were searched and terror ruled supreme. Domka Munda and Majhia Munda, the two leading Munda Sardars, surrendered along with their 32 supporters on January 28, 1900, but Birsa himself was still at large. Two search parties in Ranchi and one in Singhbhum were trying to apprehend him. Forbes, the Commissioner, asked the Rajas of Surguja, Udaipur, Jashpur and Bonai to help in apprehending Birsa. A descriptive roll of Birsa was sent to the Magistrate of Raghunath Chatti, Deputy Commissioner of Sambalpur and the political agent of Chhattisgarh. A reward of Rs.500 was announced on him. Gaya Munda was captured from Itaki. Birsa was arrested from the forests of Sentra on March 3, 1900. He was arrested during his sleep. He was forthwith taken to Ranchi jail where he died of cholera on June 9, 1900. Nearly 450 of his followers were arrested. Amongst his supporters, one was sentenced to death, 39 transported for life and 23 were awarded 14 years jail term. He was just 25 years when he died but Birsa certainly achieved one thing – a regional identification and his clarion call of "Abua raj seter jana, maharani raj tundu jana (Let the kingdom of the queen end and our kingdom be established)" continued to echo in other forms.[40]

Significance of Ulgulan

In Chota Nagpur the Birsaite movement prodded the colonial administrators into introducing long overdue reforms. Fr. Hoffmann wrote to the Commissioner that many of the complaints of the tribals were just. Two things which were most difficult but very necessary, had to be done. The codification, i.e. the legal recognition of the customs and rights proper to the tribals, and the agricultural measurements by which the rights of each farmer to the fields cultivated by him were to be accurately measured and marked on the maps. In 1902, an extensive survey of cultivated lands in Munda areas was undertaken which was designed to formally determine and record Munda land rights and obligations to landlord groups. Two British administrators played an important role in this exercise. Lister, who belonged to Indian Civil Service, was appointed Land Management Officer. Lister collected the land documents of the area and examined them. The documents of other regions of Chotanagpur were collected and examined by Reid. The joint report of the two officers was placed before the government in 1912. As a consequence, the traditional rights of the Mundas, including their ownership of Bhuinhari and Khuntkatti lands were restored.[41]

Another important step was the enactment of Chota Nagpur Tenancy Act in 1908 which established detailed regulations concerning tenant rights and obligations. The provisions of the Act placed obstacles in the process of transferring adivasi land to non-tribals. In this same period, the Government of India also abolished longstanding landlord demands for labour services to be performed by their Munda tenants (beth-begari). To insure that these new regulations were followed, the British established new courts and administrative divisions.[42]

NATURE OF ULGULAN

The second phase of Birsa movement was clearly political. In this phase, religion and politics were confusedly intermingled. The early Birsa was non-violent, but the later Birsa was a revolutionary rebel. The tenets of Birsa Dharam were formulated during the first phase of the movement. This dharma was a queer assimilation of Sarna Dharma, Hinduism and Christianity. This was an act of unison against economic exploitation. Opposition to the Christian missionaries and the government was based on these basic postulates. Inclusion of divine concepts and the transformation of Birsa himself into Bhagwan gave the movement a Messianic character. His religion was also revivalist and reformative in nature. His followers, like himself, believed in selfless service of the Munda society. Magic, witchcraft, taboos, totems and sacrifices were to be eschewed as the bane of tribal society. Economic deprivation and political subservience were equally unacceptable.[43]

Birsa Bhagwan had his own way of propagating the new faith: prediction, song and dance, meeting and discourses. Like Chaitanya Mahaprabhu, he sang and danced along with his followers. He made utterances on perennial theological concepts like the day of judgement, unflinching faith in God and complete submission to him. In keeping with tradition of pilgrimages in all principal religions of the world, he fixed the places of Birsaite pilgrimages at Chutia, Doisa, Jagannathpur, Nagpheni, Chalkad etc.[44]

There was also a tinge of magical as well as rational nativism. This aspect of Birsa dharma was manifested in his assuming the role of prophet and using supernatural techniques like use of mantra, driving away the ghosts, curing the sick, reviving the dead, his proclamations of the coming of the deluge, rain of fire, going to the sky (Sirma Disum) as Hanuman, his body turning into gold and lastly, his becoming the Dharti Aba. Birsa's claim that the bullets used against him would turn into water and only a log of wood would remain in the jail in his place were further proofs of his religion's nativism. The organizational set-up of Birsa dharma drew heavily from Christianity. Here also were the pracharaks, a book of prayer and a band of devoted disciples. Birsa, however, had neither the time nor the resources to consolidate the organization he had built up. After his death, it virtually collapsed.[45]

A group of scholars also argue that Birsa's Ulgulan had a tinge of proto-nationalism or anti-colonial utopia. This conception is based on the fact that Birsa's 'real enemies [were] the saheblok [white folk] and the Government.'[46] The lines of approach to the nature of the Ulgulan have been shifting. The description of Birsa Munda himself ranged from 'a fanatic'[47], 'an infatuated youth, a young monkey', 'a dangerous agitator, a pseudo prophet and a false messiah'[48] on the one hand to a prophet, a God, a fighter for freedom, a martyr, a great leader, who championed 'the cause of the suffering fellow beings against the grinding maladies of an offensive agrarian system and other abuses'[49] and 'led a humanitarian campaign of relieving the misery of masses and securing justice to them'[50] on the other.[51] The extent of the Ulgulan is variously described. On the one hand, Dr. Notrott, the German missionary would not even call it a Munda uprising because the entire Munda population was not involved in it, and only a very small part of it, ten to fifteen thousand, had participated.[52]The newspaper Pioneer also did not considered the matter very serious; 'the Mundas were impulsive and with their outmoded weapons they could not even face a small military force.[53]On the other hand, to the Calcutta newspapers the agrarian rising had taken a serious turn.[54]

There were millennial dreams. The ideal order, i.e. Birsa's Raj and religion, would witness the liquidation of the enemies, the dikus, the European missionaries and officials, and the native Christians. The Mundas would recover their lost kingdom. There would be enough to eat, and no famine, the people would live together and in amity. Birsa and his followers held meetings at secret and selected sites, composed prayers and incantations and prescribed and practiced rituals to destroy their enemies and put an end to the British Raj and Mandodari's (British Queen's) kingdom. From the historical standpoint Birsa and his followers have attained the status of martyrs and even today in folk songs and anecdotes their memory lingers. His considerable popularity in some Indian nationalist circles in the late 1930s was demonstrated by the gate erected in his honour at the annual Congress session in 1940 at Ramgarh, where he was proclaimed a champion in the fight against the British.[55]

NOTES AND REFERENCES

1.   Chaudhuri, B.B. 'Revaluation of Tradition in the Ideology of the Radical Adivasi Resistance in Colonial Eastern India, 1855-1932: Part II', *Indian Historical Review*, 37(1), 2010, pp.39-62

2.   De, Debasree. *Gandhi and Adivasi*, 2022, New Delhi, p17.

3.   Kalapura, Jose. *Christian Missions in Bihar and Jharkhand till 1947: A Study by P.C. Horo*, New Delhi, 2014, p.xli.

4.   Mahto, S. *Hundred Years of Christian Missions in Chotanagpur since 1845*, The Chotanagpur Christian Publication House, Ranchi, 1971, p. 37.

5.   Kalapura, Jose. op. cit. pp. xli-xlii

6.   Peter Tete S.J. *A Missionary Social Worker in India: Fr. J.B. Hoffmann*, Roma, 1984, p.26.

7.   ibid, p.93.

8.   Kalapura, Jose. op. cit. p. xlii.

9.   Mahto, S. op. cit. p.93.

10. Singh, K.S. *Tribal Movements in India*, vol. II, Manohar, New Delhi, 2006, pp.1-2.

11. Rana, L.N. "Political Consciousness in Jharkhand, 1900-1947", *Proceedings of the Indian History Congress*, vol. 57 (1996), pp. 467-484.

12. Kumar, N. *Bihar District Gazetteers: Ranchi*, Government of Bihar, Patna, 1970, pp.583-584.

13. Rana, L.N. op. cit. pp.468.

14. Wallace, Anthony. "Revitalization Movements", *American Anthropologist*, vol. 58, 1956, pp. 264-81.

15. Virottam, B. *Religious History of the Chotanagpur Tribes*, Himalaya Publishing House: Mumbai, 2020, p.121.

16. Hodne, Olav. *L.O. Skrefsrud, Missionary and Social Reformer among the Santals of Santal Parganas: With*

Special Reference to the period between 1867 and 1881, Oslo, 1966, p. 270.

17. Letter dated 7th October 1874 from G.N. Barlow, Officiating Commissioner, Santal Parganas to the Secretary, Political Department, Government of Bengal.

18. Fuchs, Stephens. *Rebellious Prophets*, Bombay, 1965, p. 53.

19. Ibid, p.53.

20. Mathur, L.P. Tribal Revolts in India under British Raj, Aavishkar Publishers: Jaipur, 2004, pp. 72-73.

21. Sinha, S.P. *Conflict and Tension in Tribal Society*, Concept Publishing Company: New Delhi, 1993, p.203.

22. Mathur, L.P. op. cit. p. 73.

23. Letter dated 8th November 1880 from Father L.O. Skresfrud to the Editor, *The Statesman and Friend of India* cited in S.P. Sinha, Conflict and Tension in Tribal Society, Concept Publishing Company: New Delhi, 1993, p.216.

24. Shukla, P.K. "Tribal Resistance in Chotanagpur: A Case Study of the Dubia Gossain Movement (1870-80)." *Proceedings of the Indian History Congress*, vol. 62, 2001, pp. 613-20.

25. MacDougall, John. "Agrarian reform vs. Religious Revitalization: Collective Resistance to Peasantization among the Mundas, Oraons and Santals, 1858-95", *Contribution to Indian Sociology*, vol.11, no.2 (1977), pp.295-321.

26. Singh, K.S. *Birsa Munda and His Movement 1874-1901: A study of a Millenarian Movement in Chotanagpur*, Oxford University Press: Calcutta, 1983, p. 30.

27. There is no unanimity among historians regarding the year and place of birth of Birsa. The dates for Birsa's birth range between 1872 and 1875, and two places, Ulihatu and Chalkad, vie in the popular imagination as his true birthplace.

28. Virottam, B. op. cit. pp.122-123.

29. Singh, K.S. *Birsa Munda and His Movement 1874-1901: A study of a Millenarian Movement in Chotanagpur*, Oxford University Press: Calcutta, 1983, p. 40.

30. Chandra, Uday. "Flaming fields and Forest Fires: Agrarian transformations and the making of Birsa Munda's rebellion", The Indian Economic and Social History Review, vol.53, 2016, pp.1-30.

31. Roy, S.C. *The Mundas and their Country*, Calcutta, 1912, p. 326.

32. Virottam, B. op. cit. p. 124.

33. Singh, K.S. op. cit. pp. 50-51.

34. Dhan, A.K. *Birsa Munda*, Publication Division, Ministry of Information and Broadcasting, Government of India: New Delhi, 2020, Kindle edition, p.1215.

35. Hoffmann J. Encyclopedia Mundarika, 1930, vol. II, p.568.

36. Bengal Police Abstract, vol. 8, Calcutta, 14th December 1895, No. 17, para 1674.

37. Meena, K.P. *Adivasi Vidroh*, Anugya books: Delhi, 2021, p. 93.

38. Peter Tete, S.J. *A Missionary Social Worker in India*, Roma, 1984, p.48.

39. Singh, K.S. *The Dust storm and the Hanging Mist*, Calcutta, 1966, pp.109-110.

40. Goswami, P. *Untold Story of Chota Nagpur: Its Journey with the Colonial Army: 1767-1947*, Chennai, 2020, p.87.

41. Dhan, A.K. op. cit. p.1183.

42. Adas, Michael. *Prophets of Rebellion: Millenarian Protest Movements against the European Colonial Order*, The University of North Carolina Press: Chapel Hill, 1979, p.178.

43. Virottam, B. op. cit. p. 127

44. ibid p. 127

45. ibid p. 128.

46. Chandra, Uday. op. cit. p.25.

47. 'Arrest of a fanatic named Birsa Munda', Proceedings nos. 38-46, Nov. 1895, Judicial Department, Government of Bengal (West Bengal State Archives, Kolkata)

48. 'News from Murhu', Quarterly Papers, S.P.G. Mission, July-Oct. 1895, p.4.

49. Datta, K.K. *History of the Freedom Movement in Bihar*, vol. 1, Patna, 1957, p.105.

50. Mazumdar, R.C. *History of the Freedom Movement in India*, vol. 1, Calcutta, 1962, p.284.

51. Singh, K.S. *Birsa Munda and His Movement 1874-1901: A study of a Millenarian Movement in Chotanagpur*, Oxford University Press: Calcutta, 1983, p. 4.

52. *The Statesman*, 2 April 1900, p.9, Dr. A. Notrott's letter to the Editor.

53. *The Pioneer*, 15 Jan. 1900.

54. *The Englishman*, 15 Jan. 1900, p.6.

55. Sinha, S.P. *The Life and Times of Birsa Bhagwan*, Ranchi, 1964, pp. iv-v.

CHAPTER IV

GOING THE GANDHIAN WAY

After the death of Birsa Munda, his movement virtually came to an end. But Birsa and his followers had prepared the soil for a greater national movement under the leadership of Mahatma Gandhi. Long before Mahatma Gandhi could give the Indians the weapons of Satyagraha and Ahimsa, the Mundas acted as the forerunners of the Non-violent revolutionary movement against the oppression of zamindars, Padris and Sarkars.[1] However, the advent of Indian National Congress on the political forefront gave a new impetus to the national movement in Chotanagpur. A large number of delegates of Chotanagpur participated in the annual sessions of Congress particularly the 27th session of Congress held at Bankipur (Bihar).

Along with the Congress, Chotanagpur became one of the important centres of revolutionary movements under the guidance of Ganesh Chandra Ghosh. On account of its geographical position and easy communications with Calcutta through Manbhum, Ranchi naturally received some impact of the revolutionary movement taking place in Bengal. Some revolutionary suspects such as Hemanta Kumar Bose, P.N. Bose and Rajat Nath Roy stayed in Ranchi in 1913.[2]

In January 1913, it was reported that seditious leaflets with heading "*Our Swadhin Bharat*" were found posted on the lamp posts in Giridih of Hazaribagh district. These leaflets were brought to Giridih by Jibon Kristo Roy, s/o Indu Bhushan Roy of 24 Parganas, and were posted by Nirmal Chandra Banerjee s/o Abinash Chandra Banerjee of Giridih.[3]

Some students of St. Columbus College, Hazaribagh were also associated with the revolutionaries. On December 13, 1918, Ram Binod Singh, a student of the college and son of a Police employee Jai Kisan Singh was arrested. Ram Binod Singh was considered as "Jatin Bagha" of Hazaribagh and so students of Hazaribagh including Bajrang Sahay and Krishna Ballabh Sahay expressed their great resentment on his arrest.[4]

The D.I.G. of Police, Crime and Railways informed to the Chief Secretary of Bihar and Orissa on October 12, 1916 that a great number of Bengali youths were working in the Chemical Department of Tata. Some of them like Durga Das Banerjee were suspects of Alipore Conspiracy Case. Therefore, the government warned the Tata Management not to employ Bengal youth without proper verification. Many of the revolutionaries associated Hindustan Association of America had settled in Chaibasa and Jamshedpur.[5]

The Indian National Movement took a new turn under the leadership of Mahatma Gandhi.In April 1917, Mahatma Gandhi was in Champaran and putting into effect what would be India's first lesson in Satyagraha. By 29 May 1917, Gandhi was summoned to Ranchi for meeting with the Lt. Governor of Bihar Sir Edward Albert Gait in connection with the agrarian conditions in Champaran. The Audrey House built by Capt. Hannygton had the privilege of being the site of the historic meeting between Lt. Governor and Mahatma Gandhi on 4 June 1917 and a second meeting on 22 September 1917. At Ranchi, Gandhiji was welcomed and greeted by several people including the Tana Bhagats who subsequently led the Independence movement in the plateau.[6] Historic not just for the meeting but also for the fact that 'Audrey House' signifies the 'launch pad' of Gandhi on the Indian Independence scene;

for the announcement and possibly success of Satyagraha as a model and most importantly for the clarion call indicating the 'final push' to independence.[7]

When the First World War came to an end, victory celebrations were sponsored by the government. However, the nationalist leaders boycotted such celebrations. Due to the extraordinary influence of Maulana A.K. Azad, who had been interned at Ranchi during the period, the anti-Peace celebration agitation were most successful at Ranchi. Similarly Rowlatt Satyagraha was also quite successful in Chotanagpur. Mahatma Gandhi gave a call to the nation to observe a nationwide hartal on April 6, 1919. There has been instances of individual fasting. Ramdin Pandey, teacher of local district high school of Palamau, observed fast on April 6 with his six students. Bareshwar Sahai of Ranchi distributed leaflets against the act.[8]Ranchi District Congress Committee was formed in 1920.

THE NON-COOPERATION MOVEMENT AND THE TANA BHAGAT MOVEMENT

Many Adivasis and non-Adivasis of Chotanagpur attended the special session of Congress held at Calcutta from 4 to 9 September 1920 under the Presidentship of Lala Lajpat Rai. At the call of Mahatma Gandhi, the tribes of Chotanagpur actively participated in the Non-Cooperation movement. Gandhiji himself visited Chotanagpur in 1920-21 and stayed at Bhimraj Bansidhar Modi Dhramshala at Ranchi. In the wake of Non-Cooperation movement, we see a tribal movement called the Tana Bhagat movement which became quite popular in Chotanagpur.

Tana Bhagat movement (1914-22) among the Oraons of Chotanagpur was a cultural revitalization movement in nature and was caused by the rise of political radicalism in the wake of Gandhian Non-Cooperation movement. It established a new sect, the Tana Sect, which was markedly different from the Oraon community. Though started much earlier the Tana Bhagat movement was heavily influenced by the Gandhian ideology and later participated in the non-violent Non-Cooperation movement called upon by Gandhi.

The movement was an obvious reaction to the repressive tax system brought forward by the erroneous survey and settlement in Chotanagpur region in 1902-8. The immediate targets were the landlords, moneylenders, British administrators, police and the dikus. The Oraons blamed their age-old Gods and Goddesses for all their hardships and started worshipping a new religious cult preached by the Vaishnava gurus called Bhagat in lieu of that.[9] Therefore, unlike the previous Ulgulan movement, the millenarian beliefs of Tana Bhagat leaders did not perhaps owe much to the Christian influence. The decisive influence on the comprehensive religious revitalization agenda was Vaishnava influence.

The Tana Bhagat movement was first started in April 1914 by a young Oraon called Jatra Bhagat of the village Chingri Nawatoly of Bishunpur Thana in Gumla sub-division. Jatra, at the age of 20, gave up the worship of spirits, prohibited from taking meat, liquor and forced labour. Very soon Jatra gained popularity and many Oraons of Ranchi, Palamau and Hazaribagh became his followers.[10] His cult was also called Kurukh Dharam (true religion). He formulated a rule of conduct and said that the Oraons have to give up worshipping of the spirits and instead worship the Kurukh dharam;

they have to give up animal sacrifice, meat-eating, liquor consumption, song and dance, visiting to the dormitories, wearing colourful clothes or jewellery or tattoo, and witchcraft practicing. He declared that the Oraons had to lead an ascetic life free from extravagance and luxury. Jatra asked his followers to stop tilling the fields and paying rents to the landlords and to refuse to engage themselves as labourers to any non-Oraons.[11] The movement spread like wildfire and the British police eventually arrested and imprisoned him.

The Oraons were well aware that mere religious revitalization would not help them in bringing the Oraon Raj. Thus it was from 1919 onwards that the Tana Bhagat movement developed political overtones. By January 1919, the fire of the Tana Bhagat movement became widespread and met with severe police repression. The leaders such as Shibu, Maya, Sukra, Singhia, and Debia were arrested and convicted.[12] And then the leadership was handed over to Turia Bhagat and Jitu Bhagat, who vigorously launched the campaign for non-payment of Chaukidari tax and no-rent campaign against the zamindars. These resolutions were immediately supported by the leadership of the Congress.[13]

The Deputy Commissioner of Ranchi admitted that the Non-Cooperation movement had revitalized the Tana Bhagat movement. The Tana Bhagats started attending the Congress meetings in large numbers. According to a report submitted by the SP, Ranchi on the issue of Non-Cooperation movement among the Oraons and other tribes of Ranchi from 31 January to 13 February 1921, it is evident that in these 13 days, 18 meetings were organized (esp. in the Tana Bhagat areas i.e. Mandar, Kuru, Lohardaga and Bero Police stations) where the tribals outnumbered the non-tribals.[14]

Rajendra Prasad, Mazhar-ul Haque and Motilal Nehru – all paid visit to different districts of Chotanagpur starting from Dhanbad, Hazaribagh, Jharia, Chatra and Ranchi. Under the influence of these great leaders, the Tana Bhagats started boycotting foreign clothand liquor. They also started using khadi and charkha. They also established village panchayats for arbitration of local disputes. They began to wear Gandhi caps and carrying Congress tricolour flags as a mark of protest against the colonial masters.

The Tana Bhagats refused to pay rent and chaukidari tax and declared that they will not give up their land, even if they were dispossessed by the landlord. The Superintendent of Police warned them that their refusal to pay rent would reduce the tenants to penury and starvation, but they refused to be intimidated to change their decision. They informed the SP that they would not pay more than 'three pailas of dhan' unless, otherwise ordered by their guru. They added that bhagwan, who resided inside them and whom they recognized as their only guru, forbade them to pay more. Turia Bhagat said, 'Bhagwan, who was speaking within him, declared that the land was theirs first.'[15]

By August 1921, the Non-Cooperation movement had acquired a strong hold among the Hos. Phulchand Dusadh, an influential person from Chittimitti, showed the villagers picture of Mahatma Gandhi and told them that Gandhi was their Raja.[16] He said: "If the people do not obey Gandhi's orders devils will come and eat them, people will get no food or drink, they will become lame...The English are leaving the country and the few Englishmen who are left behind, are hiding in Chaibasa and will run away in three or four months' time...New schools will be constructed with the order of

Gandhi and the government schools will be abolished. No school fees should be paid. The cutcheries should be closed. In Gandhi's Raj, no rents will be paid. There will be only a poll tax of two pieces per head, of which one piece will go to the Manki and the other piece to the Munda."[17]

The Khilafat Non-Cooperation movement provided an opportunity to the Tana Bhagats to vent their anger against the banias. The Tana Bhagats attempted to regulate prices and to close down large markets in some areas. In Palkot market, in February 1921, they issued orders that rice to be sold at 16 seers per rupee instead of eight, paddy at 32 seers and cloth at half price.[18]

An incident of 'looting and uproar' was reported from a market in Lohardaga in April 1921. The banias of this market purchased locally produced goods from Tendar and sold them at Lohardaga and other areas at exorbitant prices. A few days before the looting, the villagers decided at a meeting that if at the next haat the banias sold the local goods at higher prices to make a huge profit, they would beat them. Many villagers came to the haat 'armed with sticks' on the day of looting. They found to their dismay that the banias had bought up the entire stock of ploughshares. The local price of a ploughshare was 7 annas, whereas at Lohardaga it was sold for Re.1, which meant at a profit of more than 100 per cent. The stalls of the banias and other vendors were looted. Several banias were badly beaten. Grain, salt, tobacco, cloth, utensils, spice and thread disappeared from the haat. In the midst of their looting, they shouted that the British Raj was over and Gandhi was in power. The Congress leaders of Lohardaga condemned such looting and appealed to the people to adhere to non-violence.[19]

Ghani Singh Kharwar of Palamau attended the Calcutta session of Congress in 1920. After returning from the session, he organised the Kharwar tribes of Palamau for the non-cooperation movement. Under his leadership, thousands of 'reserved' Sal trees were cut and forests were cleared to prepare fields to grow cotton. Ghani Singh declared himself as the Raja of Palamau. But soon he was prosecuted by the British forces.[20] Firangi Kherwar and Parmeshwar Barhi were actively involved in the non-payment of rent propaganda in the government estate. In Khas Mahal, the campaign focused on the issue of non-payment of rent.[21]

The struggle over forests was a significant aspect of the Non-Cooperation movement in Chotanagpur. Many Kherwars participated in this movement demanding the restoration of the customary rights of tribals to extract timber and collect forest produce for their own consumption. In fact, Swaraj meant to them the restoration of their right to the forests. Tribals began to cut down the jungles on the grounds that only they were entitled to these jungles. There were cases of 'illicit cutting' in the government reserved forests. The hill side jungle in Ranka was cleared for jhum cultivation.[22]

After the suspension of the Non-Cooperation movement, Gandhi's constructive programme became the sole objective to pursue. The constructive programme were quite popular in Chota Nagpur. The 37th Annual Session of Congress was held at Gaya in December 1922. About 400 aboriginals, men and women, went to Gaya on foot.[23] P.C. Mitra, Gulab Tiwari and others held meetings at different places to collect fund for Tilak Swaraj Fund and enlisting volunteers. In the meantime there was a heroic Satyagraha at Nagpur to defend the honour of India's National flag in which Tana Bhagats from Ranchi participated.

In 1925 Gandhi visited Jamshedpur along with Dr. Rajendra Prasad at the request of C.F. Andrews and from there he went to Chaibasa, the Ho heartland and to Khunti, the Munda centre. The Hos styled themselves as the disciples of Gandhi and used to recite *Angrez Bahadur Noy* (No More British) *Gandhi Mahto Ki Jai* (Victory to Gandhi Mahto) and thus promoted Gandhi as a tribal functionary.[24] Gandhi's tour encouraged the Adivasis and the Congress leadership in organizing khadi exhibitions and popularized the use of khaddar. In 1927, Gandhi visited Chota Nagpur again and addressed a number of public meetings. Gandhi himself wrote:

"It was at Chaibasa that I made the acquaintance of the Ho tribe – a most interesting body of men and women, simple as children...Many of them have taken to the charkha and khaddar...Many have given up eating carrion and some have even taken to vegetarianism. The Mundas are another tribe whom I met at Khunti on my way to Ranchi...Among these tribes there is a quite a colony of them called Bhaktas, literally meaning devotees. They are believers in khaddar. Men and women ply the charkha regularly...They have their own bhajans which they sing in chorus. "[25]

The Bhagats used to sing songs like:

Charkha biurbiur-te,Swarajemagukeda,

Gandhian agukeda,

Sutamtakuitakute,Swarajemagukeda,

Gandhian agukeda(a Mundari bhajan)

[English translation: By spinning charkha, you bring Swaraj,

O, Gandhi, you'll bring it.

By spinning cotton, you bring Swaraj,

O, Gandhi, you'll bring it.][26]

Therefore, the Tana Bhagats could easily relate their desire for Oraon Raj to the Gandhian vision of self-rule and started imbibing the ideology propagated by him during the non-violent Non-Cooperation movement against the British.

After the sudden suspension of non-cooperation movement, once again we see a rise in revolutionary activities. Few younger adivasis of Chotanagpur also adopted the path of violence to achieve Swaraj. In 1927, Birendra Nath Bhattacharji, a revolutionary, was arrested from Deoghar. He was involved in the resuscitation of the Hindustan Republican Association after their setback due to the Kakori case. Two Mauser pistols and cartridges and a notebook were found in his possession. This led to the arrest of 12 more people and their conviction is what is known as the Deoghar Conspiracy Case.[27] In Daltonganj, dacoity from mail runners, on trains, snatching of weapons from police by revolutionaries also kept the forces in the area on their toes in the 1930s. A map with instructions to disconnect telegraph lines in Netarhat found in the possession of one Promotho Nath Mukharji on 16 September 1930 at Daltonganj also created anxious moments for the district administration.[28]

Meanwhile, Congress carried out constructive programmes in Chotanagpur and tried to expand its base among the adivasis. A Khadi exhibition was organized at Ranchi on October 5, 1926 by S.K. Sahay in the Arya

Samaj Hall in the presence of Rajendra Prasad. A Charkha demonstration was also organized in front of Durga Mandap to promote the Khadi work.

CIVIL DISOBEDIENCE MOVEMENT AND THE HARIBABA MOVEMENT

The Lahore Congress of 1929 had authorized the Congress Working Committee to launch a programme of civil disobedience including non-payment of taxes. In mid-February 1930, at a meeting at Sabarmati Aashram it invested Gandhiji with full powers to launch the Civil Disobedience movement at the time and place of his choice. Gandhi's ultimatum of 31 January to Lord Irwin stating his 11 demands had been ignored. The only way left out for Gandhiji was civil disobedience. He believed that the Salt tax constituted 'the most inhuman poll tax the ingenuity of man can devise.' Therefore, Gandhiji started his famous Dandi March to break the salt law.

Gandhiji, on 6th April 1930, by picking up a handful of salt, inaugurated the Civil Disobedience Movement. So far, as Chotanagpur is concerned, the participation of tribals was overwhelming from the very beginning. On 26th January 1930, Independence Day was celebrated and 225 Tana Bhagats participated enthusiastically in the long procession at Ranchi, shouting 'Vande Mataram' and 'Bharat Mata Ki Jai'. Dr. P.C. Mitra, the President of Ranchi District Congress Committee hoisted the national flag at the junction of three roads near the Sadar Hospital amidst great rejoicing. According to police report, subsequently 1763 Tana Bhagats had enlisted themselves as Congress members under their leader Bhuka Bhagat.[29]

At the same time, a reform movement called Sacred Thread movement was going on among the Santals of Gomia under the leadership of Bonga Manjhi of Horobera (Hazaribagh), claiming to be a disciple of Gandhiji. He asked his followers to give up non-vegetarian food and alcohol and to wear the sacred thread like the high caste Hindu. He declared that Gandhi Raj would replace the British Raj. He advised his followers to wear Khadi. The Santals refused to pay Chaukidari tax and danced under the national flag. Bangam Manjhi was arrested on 4th July 1930 and was charged with inciting the tribals against the British government.[30]

It is significant to note that during the Civil Disobedience Movement, the tribals stopped paying all taxes to the Government. The Congress volunteers often took help of some drama and song patriotic songs in the local dialects in order to bring the movement to the grass root level.[31] Dr. P.C. Mitra, after having long discussions in context to Salt Satyagraha with Deokinandan Lal, Gulab Tiwari, Nagarmal Modi, Jagadish, Charwa Bhagat, Madhu Bhagat and Ramchandra Prasad decided to make salt out of 'rehra mati' (rock salt) with the help of the Tana Bhagats of Khunti.[32]

The Congress also organized a series of forest satyagrahas demanding the tribal customary right to use timber, roots, fruits, honey etc. for their livelihood. 'Forest Satyagraha' – the reassertion by poor peasants and tribals of traditional customary rights over forests 'reserved' by the colonial state – represents an almost forgotten but fascinating aspect of Gandhian era.[33]A batch of ten Ho volunteers under the leadership of Harihar Mahto violated the forest act on 6th August 1930 by cutting down about hundred Sal trees in Lepungbera forest at the distance of about seven miles from

Chakradharpur. Soon the situation became alarming in the district and to curtail it the administration swung into action. Harihar Mahto was arrested and imprisoned. A congress worker Hari Singh was also arrested in connection with forest Satyagraha. He was imprisoned for one year and fined rupees twenty. Another forest Satyagraha was organized among the Kharwars of Palamau under the leadership of Jadubans Sahay and some other Congress leaders.[34]

The Paharias (a hill tribe) of Santhal Parganas district actively participated in the civil disobedience movement. In September 1930, Pandra Paharia of Pangropahar was prosecuted for his involvement in the movement. He was found disseminating the Congress programme in Damin area of Rajmahal. Sundra Paharia of Chandra in Godda sub-division moved about delivering speeches and asking Paharias and Santals to join the Congress movement. In October and November 1930, the Santals fought a pitched battle with a contingent of the armed police near Godda which resulted in numerous casualties on both the side and arrest of 57 persons.[35]

In Palamau district, civil disobedience began with asking people not to pay any rent including the chaukidari tax in January 1932. Bhubaneshwar Chaubey delivered a lecture to this effect in a meeting at Bishrampur. The tribal participation was encouraging in the district. Sheocharan Kharwar, a Congress tribal worker of Bhandaria was a notable figure. A meeting was held on 19 June 1932 at Nowka (Bhandaria) attended by 3000 people mostly the Kharwar tribals of Ranka and Chainpur ward estate. Voice was raised against the oppression of British Raj. Later on 27 persons were arrested by the police in connection of this meeting. Again a similar meeting was held at Chinia on 22 June 1932. In the meeting, Janaki Kharwar of Champa Kali asked the audience to obey the orders of Gandhiji. After the meeting the crowd moved in procession and proceeded towards the Congress office at Nowka Bhandaria under the leadership of Sheocharan Kharwar. At about 5 p.m. they hoisted the national flag in front of the Congress office. They established a parallel *Thana* of their own and appointed Manu Singh of Mahuadanr and Sheocharan Kharwar of Nowka as *Congress Darogas*.[36]

Meetings were again held at Garbandh and Chinia on 23 and 25 June 1932 respectively. These meetings called the Swaraj Meetings attended mostly by the Adivasis turned the situation at Bhandaria very serious for the government. An armed force under Sergeant Major English was sent to Bhandaria who brought the situation under control there. But the arrest of a prominent Adivasi leader Bandhan Kharwar on 25 June 1932 created a major trouble again. The villagers mostly Kharwars attacked the Untari police station and assaulted the policemen with lathis and other weapons. Raja of Untari, Bhaiya Sahib, reached the place of occurrence and rescued the police. On receipt of information S.P. and S.D.O. reached there with police force but by that time the villagers had already left the place. The police raided the neighbouring villages and arrested sixty-seven persons by 28 June 1932. However Bandhan Kharwar could not be arrested.[37]

In the early 1930s, a major religious reform movement began among the Hos. The movement was led by Duka Ho, who called himself as Haribaba. In spite of being primarily a religious movement, Haribaba also had a political motive. Haribaba movement swept through northern parts of Singhbhum and the whole of the Ranchi district. Though originally he hailed from Siriapos village in Seraikela estate, Haribaba erected his ashram in the forest at Jamrogara, near Chitpil which was located twelve miles north-west of Chakradharpur. The principal object of the movement was to purify Ho culture by eliminating all alien elements from its society. The Hos realized that their gods are displeased from them and therefore are not responding to their call. So, their religion required purification and reform.[38] The movement was thus against the evil practices of the Hos themselves, for example, witchcraft, black magic, blind faith on the bongas or malevolent spirits, etc.[39] The Haribabaites worshipped Hanuman and wore the sacred thread. Eating beef was strictly prohibited and vegetarianism was adopted.

The followers of Haribaba were instructed to worship the tulsi plant and wear the sacred thread. Haribaba's wife Nani Kui, known as Harima, used to sprinkle holy water on the followers on payment of a nominal fee.

According to a highly practised ceremony among tribes, the father in a family would collect some rice, make them up into three packets, one each for Gandhi, Kali and Durga, leave these packets by the side of a tank for a short while, throw Gandhi's packet into water and pick up the other two remaining packets; no explanation of this strange practice could be obtained.[40] Haribaba declared that if the Hos followed his teachings and worshipped according to his instructions, they would be able to achieve Swaraj and regain their traditional rights. Haribaba also promised that a great meeting attended by himself, Tara Chand (another Tribal leader) and Gandhi would be held on some hill near Jamshedpur, and that the state of things as existed before the British Raj would be restored.

The British authority kept a close watch on the movement. On 27 July 1931, Haribaba was arrested on charges of sedition. After Haribaba's imprisonment, his wife Nani Kui tried to keep the movement alive. She set an ashram at Nandpur near Manoharpur and preached Haribaba's spiritual purification teachings. A disciple of Haribaba named Jojo Tamaria preached on his line but soon Nani Kui along with Jojo Tamaria were also arrested. Eventually, the British repression succeeded in quelling the movement and the new religion of Haribaba gradually disappeared into oblivion.[41]

Another leader Silu Santal (alias Tarachand) rose at Rajbasa in Sarangpur police station in Dhalbhum. Mango leaves were circulated as far as Mayurbhanj, asking the Santals to assemble at Rajbasa for planning a revolution. On 15 May 1931 a large number of Santals did assemble there to pull down the telegraph line to show their 'independence'. In spite of the order of the authorities not to perform the charak-puja, Tarachand did it, saying that he did not care for the British soldiers for he had with him a large force without uniforms to whom guns would not do any harm.

When Haribaba started a new cult, he came into contact with Tarachand and his disciple Jaichand Santal of Dhalbhum. They planned a mass meeting with Gandhiji's blessings to restore the condition before the British raj. Tarachand assembled about four thousand tribesmen in the Kherawan state and got timber from the Government reserved forest for constructing a temple complex. He was arrested on 25 July. But Jaichand's followers beat up the police. This was followed by the arrest of eleven people including Jaichand by the British troops and the dismantling of the newly constructed temple complex.

The Post Civil Disobedience Movement Phase

People who participated in Civil Disobedience Movement became active politically and retained the spirit of activism involving themselves in constructive activities of Gandhi, such as the formation of Seva Dals, promoting Khadi and spinning, organisation of schools, struggle against untouchability upliftment of Harijans and women, boycott of foreign cloth and liquor, Hindu-Muslim unity etc. Such activities mobilize people including oppressed classes.[42] Adivasi welfare was the fourteenth item in the list of Gandhiji's constructive programme. Gandhi directed that a constructive worker should engage himself in the constructive work among the Adivasis and resort to individual civil disobedience to overcome Government's opposition to his work.[43]

Accordingly, under the instruction of Rajendra Prasad, a noble scheme was initiated in order to uplift the aboriginal tribes of Chotanagpur and Santal Parganas. A Board was formed for imparting training to the primitive and aboriginal tribes with Nibaran Dasgupta of Purulia as President. The Board consisted of Kshistish Chandra Basu of Ranchi as Secretary and Rajendra Prasad, Jeemut Bahan Sen, Saraswati Devi as members and six representatives in-charge of six districts viz. Shashi Bhushan Rai for the Santhal Pargana, K.B. Sahay for Hazaribagh, Bejoy Krishna Dutt for Ranchi, Ashwani Kumar Paul for Manbhum, Chandrika Prasad for Palamau and Ananda Kishore Lal for Singhbhum. So far as the objectives of the Board were concerned, it was decided that centre would be started in each district where tribals would receive training in:

1. Preventing evil like drinking by magic lantern lectures and other mediums of propaganda

2. Stopping litigation by organizing panchayat committee

3. Protecting themselves from the oppression of zamindars and mahajans by arousing the consciousness of their own strength

4. Primary education

5. Cotton growing, spinning and weaving

6. Lathi playing and

7. Regular volunteer corps by regular parade etc.

There was a widespread and whole-hearted participation of the Santhals of Hazaribagh, the Tana Bhagats of Ranchi and Mahtos of Manbhum at the conference at Hutmura, where this Board was formed. The Chief Secretary, Government of Bihar and Orissa found objective (3), (6) and (7) objectionable and sent notices to district officers with an instruction to keep a vigilance on this scheme. Meanwhile, Rajendra Prasad began his tour in the Santhal Parganas in order to implement this noble scheme. He drew the large audience at Pakur but elsewhere the attendance was meagre.[44]

Therefore, as Coupland remarks the constructive phase of post- civil disobedience movement has shown that the power of the great organisation of Congress and the disciplined enthusiasm of its members could be put to a more practical purpose.[45]

Meanwhile, the commencement of the Second World War influenced the course of struggle for freedom in India. The INC declared the nature of Anglo-German war as an imperialist war and it disapproved of 'the Indian troops being made to fight for Great Britain' and 'drain from India of men and material for the purpose of war.'[46]In the year 1940, the 53rd session of the INC was held at Ramgarh of Hazaribagh district on 19 March and 20 March under the leadership of Maulana Azad. In his welcome address, Rajendra Prasad recalled the glorious traditions of Bihar and observed: "Today we are to face a big crisis and we are called upon to get ready to meet it." Jawaharlal Nehru moved the resolution on Satyagraha. The resolution was seconded by Acharya Kripalani. The Ramgarh session of INC gave a clarion call to the Nation to be ready for the inevitable struggle under the leadership of Gandhi. Earlier on March 14, Mahatma Gandhi opened the Khadi and Village Industries Exhibition at Ramgarh.

Some Indian nationalists of radical political views, mostly of the Forward Bloc (formed by S.C. Bose) and Radical Democratic Party (founded by M.N. Roy), were not in agreement with the Congress standpoint regarding the war crisis. They held All India Anti-Compromise Conference at Ramgarh during the Congress session under the Presidentship of Subhash Chandra Bose. They demanded that there should be no compromise with the imperialist forces. Swami Sahajanand Saraswati, Shilbhadra Yajee and some others played a prominent role in it.[47]

But the setback to France in June 1940 and consequently the impending danger of the Nazi invasion made the Congress Working Committee realise that 'the problem of the achievement of national freedom has now to be considered along with the one of its maintenance and defence of the country against the possible external and internal disaster.'[48] Gandhiji found the August Offer of Viceroy Linlithgow, announced on 8 August 1940 and which envisaged that after the war a representative body of Indians would be set to frame the new constitution, to be unsatisfactory. So, he decided to launch Individual Satyagraha on 17th October 1940. It was decided that the campaign should be limited to selected individuals because neither the Congress nor Gandhi wanted the war effort to be seriously hampered by a mass movement. The Satyagraha was intended to disapprove the British claim that India was whole-heartedly helping the war effort. The first Satyagrahi selected was Acharya Vinoba Bhave, second was J.L. Nehru and third was Brahma Dutt. From Chotanagpur, a number of tribal leaders were selected as the Satyagrahis. Gandolal Paharia staged Satyagraha in Pakur sub-division and shouted anti-war slogans. He was arrested under Defence of India Regulations and sentenced to four months rigorous imprisonment. Maisa Paharia, Ulfat Hussain, Bhim Kisku, Rupnath Mahto, Nilkanth Thakur and Dev Chand Noonia joined the Individual Satyagraha in Godda sub-division. They were arrested and sentenced to six weeks rigorous imprisonment and a fine of Rs. five.[49]

QUIT INDIA MOVEMENT AND TRIBAL PARTICIPATION IN CHOTANAGPUR

In the Quit India movement, the Adivasi participation was spectacular. Lakshiram Hembrom, a Santhal leader, led the rebels to burn down many liquor shops. In the summer of 1942, Rajendra Prasad and Krishna Singh visited Chota Nagpur and played a key role in preparing the background of Quit India Movement. On 14 August 1942, the students of the district school of Ranchi started the Quit India Movement by taking out a procession. On 17 August 1942, a procession was taken out in Ranchi. In this procession, the treasurer of Congress Committee of Ranchi, Sheo Narain Modi was arrested. On 18 August, Tana Bhagats burnt Bishunpur police station. On 22 August, in Ranchi, P.C. Mitra was arrested. The agitators uprooted the rail track and telegraph wires between Itki and Tangarbaisti on 23rd August.[50]

On 11 August 1942, the movement started under the leadership of Saraswati Devi in Hazaribagh. Workers working in the mines of Mica took out a procession in Jhumri Tilaiya, in which 113 people were arrested and a procession was also taken out in Domchang, on which police opened fire killing two people and injuring twenty- two others. In Jamshedpur, mill workers and businessmen organized a full strike on 10 August, 1942. Prominent agitators M.K. Ghosh, M. John, N.N. Banerjee, Treta Singh, and T.P. Sinha etc. were arrested.[51]

The movement in Palamau started on 11 August. The prominent leaders who led this movement were Yadunandan Tiwari, Jaganarayan Pathak, Mahavir Verma, Yaduvansha Sahay, Gauri Shankar Ojha, Rajeshwari Saroj Das etc. On 17 August, tribals agitated in Daltonganj in which Vishnu Prasad, Ganauri Singh were arrested. They both were sentenced to one year imprisonment. On 1 September, Girijanand Singh was arrested in Latehar and sentenced to one year imprisonment. A meeting was held under the leadership of Vinodanand Jha at Deoghar in Santhal Pargana. The national flag was hoisted at Godda office on 15 August and the protestors destroyed railway tracks, wires and telephone lines. The movement was further intensified with the joining of Santhal and Pahariya tribes in large numbers. Many women, students and tribals were arrested under the India Security Act.[52]

On 25 August, tribals set fire to the buildings of Dak Bungalow and Forest Department in Alubera. Police fired on the agitators in which Trigunanand Khabare was killed. Gandemal Paharia, Babulal Maraiya, Kartik Grihi and Shyam Tudu had burnt the Alubera Dak Bungalow. On 15th March 1943 they were sentenced to three years' imprisonment and a fine of Rs. Fifty each. Kartik Grihi who was a resident of village Telopara under Bungalow Bokrabandh in Godda Damin area, could not bear the atrocities committed against his co-prisoners and went on a hunger strike to protest against the jail authorities of Dumka jail. On 23rd March 1943, he died in Pakur jail.[53]

Several national leaders arrested from the country were brought to Hazaribagh jail during the Quit India Movement, with the most prominent socialist leader being Jai Prakash Narayan. On 8 November 1942, on the eve of Diwali, Jai Prakash Narayan, Yogendra Shukla, Suryanarayan Singh, Gulali Prasad, Shaligram Singh and Ramanand Mishra escaped from Hazaribagh jail.[54]

In 1942 and 1943 the followers of 'sapha hors' movement took an active part in the Quit India movement. For several acts of sabotage some of them were imprisoned.Ghanshyam Ojha, a Congress worker from Daltonganj, while mobilising the Kharwars in the course of the 1942 movement advocated forcible cutting away of lac by tenants, abolition of zamindari, etc. It appears from the records that Kharwars' involvement in the 1942 movement was next only to the Tana Bhagats' in its intensity.[55]Jadubans Sahay, a distinguished Congress leader organised the Kharwar and Parahias to participate in the freedom movement. Bhagirith Singh, a Kharwar, rose to be the Secretary of District Congress Committee, and was sentenced to rigorous imprisonment for reviving the Kharwar agitation in the 1940s. He also organised melas in honour of the Kharwar freedom fighters of 1857, Nilambar and Pitambar.[56]

The Quit India Movement started by Gandhi in August 1942 had placed a major challenge for the British. Gen. Slim, then responsible for internal security in Bengal writes, "The Congress party, by far the most powerful political party in India, was rapidly working up anti-Allied feeling. It not only urged all Indians to refrain from the war effort, but its agents conducted a campaign against recruiting, and attempted to suborn sepoys from their allegiance."[57] Slim noted "They took the form of concerted attacks on strategic rail communications. Large gangs, numbering often several hundreds, armed with primitive but effective weapons and some fire arms, assaulted railway stations all over the country."[58]

One of the distinguishing features of the Quit India movement was that the mass upsurge was accompanied by a fairly well-organised underground resistance movement and setting up of parallel governments. A parallel government also worked at Sarwan for some time under Prafulla Chandra Patnaik.[59] Prafulla Chandra Patnaik, K. Gopalan and Srikrishna Prasad of Damin-i-Koh organised the Paharias for the movement and divided them into five divisions, for procuring food, intelligence, obstructing roads, wrecking bridges and official residencies and lastly for arresting enemies. A parallel government also worked at Sarwan for some time. Babua Singh Paharia and Bhainsa Singh Paharia were brave soldiers of the party of P.C. Patnaik. On 6th November 1942, they burnt the Raxi Bunglow (Barhait) and in a fierce fight were severely wounded. They were arrested by the police, and sent to Rajmahal jail. Bara Dharma Paharia, a resident of village Telopara under Bunglow Bokrabandh in Godda Damin area, took an active part in the burning of shops and breaking of bridges. He was arrested, sentenced to four years rigorous imprisonment and at the age of 34, he died in Dumka jail.[60]

The spy department of P.C. Patnaik government was effectively controlled by Jama Kumar Paharia. His political discrimination, knowledge of the region and ardent patriotism aided the work of Patnaik and his friends. Another brave spy was Singhal Mal Paharia, a resident of Sindrijola village under Bungalow Bokrabandh in Godda Damin area. He was captured with another spy Nandlal and mercilessly beaten by the police.[61]

Therefore, this chapter carefully analysed the theme of nationalist upsurge in tribal movements of Chotanagpur. In the pre-Gandhian era, Indian nationalists did not take much notice of the problems confronting the tribal people. Only when Mahatma Gandhi appeared as a Colossus on the Indian political scene, did tribal people and their problem came on the national agenda. Mahatma Gandhi's introduction with aborigines occurred in South Africa, where he witnessed the people of 'Zulu' tribe and described them as 'innocent and ignorant people'[62]. His encounter with Indian tribes was at Chotanagpur when he came in contact with his 'most worthy disciples' the Tana Bhagats.Thus this chapter argues that in the tribal movements of Chotanagpur that occurred in the Gandhian era, certain new characteristics emerged, which marked a departure from earlier tribal revolts. The new tribal movements came to be led by non-tribal nationalist leaders and the methods mostly used were non-violent Satyagraha. Besides, new movement succeeded in establishing a new linkage between local issues and the rising wave of national consciousness. A large number of tribals joined the

Gandhian movement and participated both in combative and constructive programmes launched by Gandhi.

NOTES AND REFERENCES

1. Sinha, S.P. "The First Birsaite Uprising 1895", *Journal of Bihar Research Society*, vol. XLV, Part I-IV, December 1959, p.402.

2. Bihar and Orissa-Police Abstract of Intelligence (Ranchi), No. 1249 dated 1.11.1913; No. 1399 dated 29.11.1913 and No. 1956 dated 15.11.1914. Cited in S. Mishra, "History of the Freedom Movement in Chotanagpur", Patna, 1990, pp.12-13.

3. ibid pp. 46-47.

4. Ibid pp. 47-48.

5. Veerottam, B. *Jharkhand: Itihaas evam Sanskriti*, Patna, 2001, pp.352-353.

6. Kumar, N. *Bihar District Gazetteers: Ranchi*, 1970, Patna, p.75.

7. Goswami, P. *Untold Story of Chota Nagpur*, Chennai, 2020, pp.93-94.

8. Bihar and Orissa Police Abstract of Intelligence, File No. 648, dated April 12, 1919.

9. De, Debasree. *Gandhi and Adivasis*, New Delhi, 2022, p. 96.

10. Dutta, K.K. *History ofFreedom Movement in Bihar*, vol. I, Patna, 1957, p. 332.

11. Phillip, Ekka. 'Revivalist Movements among the Tribals of Chota Nagpur' in *Tribal Situation in India*, ed. K.S.

Singh, Shimla: Indian Institute of Advanced Studies, 1972, p.426.

12. Letter dated 15 October 1919 from Commissioner of Chota Nagpur to Government of Bihar, Ranchi. Cited in S.P. Sinha, Conflict and Tension in Tribal Society, op. cit., pp. 261-2.

13. Dhan, R.O. 'The Problems of the Tana Bhagats of Ranchi District', *Bulletin of Bihar Tribal Welfare Research Institute*, Ranchi, vol. 2, 1960, p.169.

14. Datta, K.K. *History of Freedom Movement in Bihar*, vol. I, Patna, 1957, p. 336.

15. Bihar and Orissa Political Special File No. 50/1921, Commissioner, Ranchi to Chief Secretary, 6 March 1921.

16. Bihar and Orissa Political Special File no. 478/1921, 'From District Magistrate, Singhbhum, to Lyall, Commissioner of the Chota Nagpur Division, 2 September 1921'. Cited in De, Debasree. *Gandhi and Adivasis*, New Delhi, 2022, p. 112.

17. Ibid.

18. Singh, Lata. *Popular Translations of Nationalism Bihar, 1920-1922*, New Delhi, 2012, p. 178.

19. Ibid, pp. 178-179.

20. Veerottam, B. op. cit. p.355.

21. Singh, Lata. op. cit. p.192.

22. Ibid, pp. 192-193.

23. The *Searchlight*, December 24, 1922.

24. De, Debasree, op. cit. p. 113.

25. Quoted in K.K. Datta, *Writings and Speeches of Gandhiji Relating to Bihar from 1927 to 1947*, Govt. of Bihar, Patna, March 1967,pp. 181-2.

26. Singh, K.S. "The Mahatma and the Adivasis", *Gandhi and the Social Sciences*, 1970, pp.125-126.

27. Terrorism in India 1917-1936, Intelligence Bureau, Govt. of India Press, 1937, p. 104.

28. Ibid, p. 113-114.

29. Mishra, S. op. cit., p 23.

30. Kumar, Sanjay. "The Civil Disobedience Movement and the Tribes of Bihar (1930-33)", *JASRAE*, Vol. XII, Issue no. 23, Oct 2016, pp.544-548.

31. Jha, J.C. *The Indian National Congress and the Tribals*, New Delhi, 1985, p. 46.

32. Kumar, Sanjay. op. cit. p.545.

33. Sarkar, Sumit. "Primitive Rebellion and Modern Nationalism: A Note on Forest Satyagraha in the Non-Cooperation and Civil Disobedience Movements", *Proceedings of the Indian History Congress*, vol. 38 (1977), pp. 511-523.

34. Rana, L.N. "Politics in Jharkhand during the Civil Disobedience Movement (1930-1934)", *Proceedings of the Indian History Congress*, vol. 66 (2005-2006), pp. 1101-1118.

35. Jha, J.C. op. cit. p.52.

36. Rana, L.N. op. cit. pp.1111-1112.

37. Mishra, S. op. cit. pp.100-101.

38. De, Debasree, op. cit. p. 114.

39. Areeparampil, Mathew. 'Socio-cultural and Religious Movements among the Ho Tribals of Singhbhum District of Bihar', in *Continuity and Change in Tribal Society*, ed. Mrinai Miri, Shimla: Indian Institute of Advanced Studies, 1993, p. 399.

40. Singh, K.S. 'Haribaba and his Movement: Changes in Chota Nagpur', *Tribal Transformation in India*, vol. III in Tribal Studies of India Series, ed. Buddhadeb Chaudhury, New Delhi: Inter India Publications, 1992, pp.344-57.

41. De, Debasree, op. cit. p. 115-118.

42. Padhy, S.C. "Indian National Movement and Individual Civil Disobedience Movement: A study in Orissa Context", *Proceedings of the Indian History Congress*, vol. 65 (2004), pp. 746-760.

43. De, Debasree, op. cit. p. 93.

44. Kumar, Sanjay. "The Civil Disobedience Movement and the Tribes of Bihar (1930-33)", *JASRAE*, Vol. XII, Issue no. 23, Oct 2016, pp.544-548.

45. Coupland, R. *India, A Restatement*, pp. 165-68.

46. Padhy, S.C. op. cit. 751.

47. Diwakar, R.R. *Bihar through the Ages*, Calcutta: Orient Longmans, 1959, p. 665. See also, Sitaramayya, P.*History of Indian National Congress*, vol. II (1935-1947), New Delhi: S. Chand, 1969, pp.167-181.

48. Padhy, S.C. op. cit. 751-2.

49. Verma, D.N. "Some Unknown Paharia Freedom Fighters of Santal Parganas Division in Jharkhand state",

Proceedings of the Indian History Congress, vol.61 (2000-01), pp. 733-738.

50. Mishra, S. op cit. p 37.

51. Chopra, P.N. *Quit India Movement*, Publications Division, Govt. of India, New Delhi, 1987, pp.30-32.

52. Mishra, S. op. cit. pp.105-108.

53. Verma, D.N. op. cit. pp. 733-738.

54. Bhuyan, A.C. *The Quit India Movement*, Manas Publications: New Delhi, 1975, pp. 103-104.

55. Singh, K.S. "A Forest Satyagraha" in K.S. Singh (ed.) Tribal Movements in India, vol. II, New Delhi, p.194.

56. Ibid, p.195.

57. Slim, W.J. *Defeat into Victory: Battling Japan in Burma and India 1942-1945*, Natraj Publishers: Dehra Dun, 1981, pp. 127-128.

58. Ibid. p.136.

59. Chopra, P.N. op. cit. p.31.

60. Gupta, R. "Gumnam Paharia Swantantra Senani (1772-1942)"in Ramnika Gupta (ed.) *Adivasi Shaurya evam Vidroh (Jharkhand)*, Surbhi Publishers: Delhi, 2015, pp. 22-28.

61. Verma, D.N. op. cit. pp. 733-738.

62. Singh, K.S. "The Mahatma and the Adivasis", in Vidyarthi, L.P., Srivastava, B.R. and Sahay, B.N., *Gandhi and Social Sciences*, New Delhi, Book Hive, 1970, pp.125-126.

CHAPTER V
DEMAND FOR POLITICAL AUTONOMY

The Adivasi endorsed nationalist political ideology preached by Gandhi and participated in the nationalist struggle headed by him, but they did not forget their own demands. Swaraj for them not only meant freedom from foreign yoke, it was also from the oppression of the dikus, moneylenders and zamindars.[1]

Chotanagpur, where the tribal system had survived relatively intact, became the centre of a dynamic separatist movement due to a combination of many reasons. Firstly, Chotanagpur was the most advanced of the tribal regions in point of literacy, political consciousness and industrial progress. Secondly, the major tribal communities were concentrated in a geographically distinct region; they were not scattered. Thirdly, Christianity was a strong force in Chotanagpur; the major tribes became very effectively evangelised. Fourthly, the Chotanagpur tribes had a tradition of militant and organised struggles for land going back over a hundred years. Fifthly, there was a rich corpus of anthropological literature to draw upon in order to create a new sense of history to legitimise the tribals' search for identity.[2] Sarat Chandra Roy gave eloquent expression to the tribals' demand for separation; his ideas and draftsman-ship left their imprint on the memoranda submitted by tribal organisations before different government bodies.[3]

The assertion of political autonomy and demand for a separate state of Chotanagpur can be traced back to the beginning of twentieth century. The spread of western education produced an Adivasi elite-Christian and developed a pan-tribal sentiment in the region as well. It began with the efforts of a students' union of St. Columbus College, Hazaribagh, and an institution that became an important centre of tribal activity in the regionAs early as in December 1909, Father Hoffmann in order to improve the economic conditions of the tribals and to free them from the clutches of moneylenders had started *Chota Nagpur Catholic Cooperative Credit Society* which forwarded loans to the Adivasis.[5]

The style of politics changed considerably in the second decade of twentieth century. Neo-literates from the tribes were drawn into constitutional politics involving regular meetings, drafting of resolutions, memoranda and petitions submitted to the government, coupled with social reform and welfare activities. There was decreasing recourse to religious and community symbols, with organization and institutional politics replacing 'inspirational' modes.[6]The pioneers were J. Bartholomew and Peter Howarad who established a branch of Dacca Students Union in 1912 to deal with the problems faced by poor tribal students. The union planned and organized religious discourse, discussions and seminars, stage plays and was successful in mobilising tribal students to demand better educational facilities, economic avenues and job opportunities.[7]

Some educated Christian tribals of Lutheran mission (Germans) and Anglican Mission established the Chota Nagpur Improvement Society in Ranchi in 1915. It demanded employment for educated tribals, reservation in the services and legislative bodies and formation of a sub-state joined to Bengal or Orissa. In 1928, Chota Nagpur Improvement Society was renamed as Chota Nagpur Unnati Samaj. The party had raised the issue of separate statehood during the visit of Simon Commission in 1928.Its founder members were Joel Lakra, Anand Mashi Topno, Theble Oraon, Paul Dayal and Bandi Oraon.

The main objectives of the Samaj were to uplift Chotanagpur from its present backward state and to improve the social, political and economic conditions of the tribals of Chotanagpur.[8] These objectives were propagated through the journal *Adibasi,* which was published in English, Hindi, Kurukh and Mundari. The main slogan of this organization was "If we want to hold our own in India we must hang together or we shall be hanged separately."[9]

CHANGES MADE BY GOVERNMENT OF INDIA ACT, 1935

The colonial government followed a policy of 'divide and rule' and this tribal policy of segregation was manifested in the Scheduled District Act (1874). Behind the Government of India Act of 1919 the belief was that the tribals need special law as they are a separate ethnic community than the caste. The Simon Commission had recommended the exclusion of Chotanagpur plateau fromthe operation of reforms due to the presence of large number of tribals' there.[10]Thus the concept of the backward areas was shaped during the colonial era. Later the tribal and non-tribal areas were both partly and fully 'excluded' in the Government of India Act of 1935.[11]

The Government of India Act, 1935 which received royal assent on 2ⁿᵈ August 1935 and came into effect on 1ˢᵗ April 1937 marked a transition from the provincial dyarchy to provincial autonomy though limited in character. The Act was based on Lord Linlithgow's Joint Select Committee's analysis of the British government's 'White Paper' produced after the Round Table Conferences held between 1930 and 1932. The Act declared Chotanagpur and Santhal Parganas as "Partially Excluded Areas" of Bihar (under Section 91, Part III, Chapter V) and separated Orissa from Bihar which was constituted into a province on 1ˢᵗ April 1936.

The Act provided for the setting up of a bicameral legislature for Bihar, consisting of a Lower House (Legislative Assembly) with 152 members, all elected on a much wider franchise; and an Upper House (Legislative Council) with 30 members of whom 14 were to be directly elected, 12 elected by the Lower House and 4 nominated.

The number of Assembly constituencies in Chotanagpur and Santhal Pargana, was 38 including 17 general (2 urban and 15 rural), 4 seats reserved for scheduled Castes, *7 seats reserved for Backward Tribes*; 8 for Muhammadans; 1 for Anglo-Indian; and 2 for Europeans besides 10 special constituencies including 1 for Indian Christians; 4 Commerce and Industry, Mining and Planting; 2 Landholders; 2 Labour and 1 University. Of the 38 constituencies 9 were double member constituencies and one was a three member constituency. Therefore, total number of seats in Chotanagpur and Santhal Pargana was 49. Besides, it had 7 seats in Legislative Council comprising 4 General, 2 Muhammadan and 1 European.[12]

PROVINCIAL ELECTIONS OF 1937

The 49th Session of the Indian National Congress (April 1936) held at Lucknow and presided over by J.L. Nehru rejected the Government of India Act, 1935 but it decided to contest the elections under the Act with a purpose of combating it and seeking to end it. In his presidential address, he said: *"... the new Act...is a retrograde measure and has been condemned by even the most moderate and cautious of our politicians, what then we are to do with this new charter of slavery... We have no choice but to contest the election to the new provincial legislatures...with our demand for a Constituent Assembly in the fore-front...One of the principal reasons for our seeking election will be to carry the message of the Congress to the millions of voters and to the scores of millions of the disfranchised, to acquaint them with our future programme and policy, to make the masses realize that we not only stand for them but that we are of them and seek to cooperate with them in removing their social and economic burdens."*[13]

The election manifesto of Congress included democratic demands for civil liberties and equal rights and a social and economic programme pinpointing the appalling poverty, unemployment, rural indebtedness of the peasantry and promised labour reforms, removal of disabilities irrespective of caste, creed, sex and religion etc., removal of untouchability and encouragement of Khadi and cottage industries. The voicing of the demands of the peasants and workers played a big role in mobilising the overwhelming mass support for the Congress.[14]

Ram Narayan Singh, member of the Central Legislative Assembly, was appointed party observer and made election-in-charge of Chotanagpur by the Bihar Provincial Congress Committee (BPCC). Under his direction local Congress leaders organized meetings at different places in the area to disseminate among the people the message of the Congress as contained in the election manifesto to rally their support. Nehru, himself, in early 1937, addressed election meetings at Hazaribagh, Ranchi, Jamshedpur, Dhanbad and Jharia. He explained to the people that the ultimate aim of Congress was to achieve independence and establishment of the Panchayati Raj.Rajendra Prasad, President of BPCC and other national leaders also undertook the election tours of Chotanagpur and Santhal Pargana and left considerable psychological effects on the tribes despite the fact that most of the Congress candidates nominated to contest the elections belonged to Zamindar class.[15]

Another political party to contest the elections in 1937 was *Bihar Prantiya Kisan Sabha (BPKS)*which decided to work in collaboration with the Congress. Its basic demands were the abolition of zamindari system and the writing off the agrarian debt while its immediate demands included the abolition of rent in kind, the exemption of uneconomic holdings, cancellation of arrears and the reduction of rent. *The Depressed Class League* formed in 1935 was also in alliance with the Congress for the elections.

The close cooperation between the Congress and the BPKS was looked upon as a matter of concern by both the government and the zamindars, particularly when the elections were impending. Hence, the *United Political Party* was formed by the zamindars and was backed by the government. The then Governor of Bihar Sir James David Sifton himself invited some important zamindars of South

Bihar at Ranchi in June 1936 to discuss about the upcoming elections. Apart from this, there were three distinct Muslim parties active in the region viz. the *United Party, the Ahrar Party and the Independent Party.*

The *Chotanagpur Unnati Samaj,* was also not satisfied with just the 'partial exclusion' of Chotanagpur by the Govt. of India Act, 1935 and made the 'formation of Chotanagpur into a sub-province' an election issue and set up its candidates against the Congress nominees in the 1937 elections. Another tribal organisation, the *Chotanagpur Kisan Sabha* was formed in 1931 under the leadership of Theble Oraon on the lines of BPKS. It was an offshoot of the Unnati Samaj and acted as counterpoise to the tribal-Christians' organisations. Since its inception, it had been agitating for reduction of land rent and aimed at improving the economic and agricultural conditions of the tribal peasantry and creating better relationship between them and their landlords. It had little resources to enter the electoral fray though it sent candidates in the elections.

The *Chotanagpur Catholic Sabha* was formed in 1929 by Boniface Lakra and Ignes Beck with the encouragement and support of the Archbishop of Chotanagpur. The aim of this organisation was the promotion of socio-religious and economic advancement of Catholic converts but it also took an active interest in the politics of the area. Boniface Lakra and Ignes Beck both contested the 1937 elections and were elected. The Kisan Sabha and Chotanagpur Unnati Samaj had also contested elections but lost to the Catholic candidate due to the better organization and popularity of Catholic Mission.[16]

The elections to the Bihar Legislative Assembly and the Council tool place simultaneously between the 22nd and 29th of January 1927. The results of the elections was a sweeping victory for the Congress in the whole of the province. It captured 6 out of 7 backward tribe (Adivasi) seats, two-third of the General and the Muhammadan seats and all the scheduled castes seats. Important winners included Krishna Ballabh Sahay who was returned from Central Hazaribagh General Rural constituency, Devendra Nath Samanta was returned from Singhbhum General Rural constituency. Abdul Bari, who became Deputy Speaker of the Assembly, was elected from North Santhal Pargana Muhammadan rural constituency. Jimut Bahan Sen and Binodanand Jha were returned from Chotanagpur Division General Urban and Deoghar cum Jamtara General Rural constituency respectively.[17]

Regional tribal parties, the Chotanagpur Unnati Samaj and Chotanagpur Kisan Sabha could not win even a single seat though the Chotanagpur Catholic Sabha succeeded in winning two Assembly seats. Thus, in the Assembly elections, the tribal parties failed to record any impressive success. Their anti-Congress stance, opposition to the national movement, propagation of ethnic separatism and the rivalry among themselves for establishing supremacy in the regional politics were the main reasons for their debacle in the elections. Moreover a large number of non-Christian tribals who stuck to the Gandhian programme of nationalist stream supported the Congress in the elections.[18]

In the wake of the electoral setback in the Provincial elections of 1937 and the District Board elections of 1938, all the tribal organizations of Chota Nagpur, viz. Chota Nagpur

Unnati Samaj, Catholic Sabha and Kisan Sabha decided to unite[19] and consequently merged to form the *Adivasi Mahasabha* on 31 May 1938, under the leadership of Theodore Surin, Rai Sahib Bandi Ram Oraon and Paul Dayal at Adivasi Bhawan in Ranchi.[20] Surin and Bandi Ram Oraon were elected as President and Vice-President respectively. Paul Dayal and Joseph Topno became General Secretary and Joint Secretary. Theophil Kujur was elected cashier of the organization.[21]The purpose of this organization was to demand for a separate state for the tribals of Chota Nagpur.

The Commissioner of Chotanagpur in his fortnightly (confidential) report stated that Ram Narayan Singh, the newly elected member of the Legislative Assembly from his region had been working up a campaign to oppose the treatment of Chotanagpur under the new constitution. It seems that all political parties of Chotanagpur on this issue. The separation of Orissa from Bihar had inspired the political conscious and educated tribal leaders to demand a separate state.[22]

Two other factors which influenced the formation of Mahasabha were the Bengali-Bihari controversy and Muslim League politics. The Bengalis felt that their interests in Bihar were not safe and therefore, they should combine with the tribals to form a separate state. The Muslim League, in the mid-1940s, played with the idea of forming a corridor passing through the tribal areas to link the proposed areas which would constitute East and West Pakistan. They sympathised with, and gave financial support to Adivasi Mahasabha.[23]

Congress Ministry in Bihar 1937-39

The Congress Ministry formed under Sri Krishna Sinha in Bihar on July 20, 1937 took up a number of measures for the benefit and welfare of the tribal population of Chotanagpur. It was decided to allot, the unexpended balance of the Government of India's rural development grant i.e. Rs. 50000 or more to each district of Chotanagpur division and the Santhal Parganas for small irrigational projects and another Rs. 50000 for big irrigation projects to be spent within a year. An experiment was also initiated in establishing a graingola at a cost of Rs. 26,000 in each district of Chotanagpur to see whether the poor Adivasis could be relieved from the clutches of Mahajans with the help of the state.

Further, special efforts were made to rehabilitate Lac industry. It was an important subsidiary occupation of the agriculturalist of Chotanagpur providing them 25 per cent of their income. Besides, the Ministry year marked some amount for provision and improvement of drinking water in rural areas for the special benefit of Adivasis and Harijans. The schemes for forest development and necessary concessions to the raiyats also was crucial. The Chotanagpur Tenancy (Amendment) Act, 1938 was calculated to provide relief to tenants of Chotanagpur by reducing rents, protecting them from illegal exactions and preventing their lands from passing out of their hands.

The Congress ministry sanctioned a scheme of opening 333 new primary schools in the various districts to educate the tribal population. A sum of Rs. 10000 was granted annually on scholarships to tribal students for technical and industrial training.[24]Besides it appointed a committee to enquire into the system of administration in Chotanagpur and Santhal Parganas and to suggest such changes and improvement in it as would be conducive to the well- being of its inhabitants. The committee submitted its report to the government and special legislation to implement some of its recommendations was already under preparation when the ministry finally resigned on 31 October 1939 in the wake of the outbreak of Second World War and the changing political situation in the country.[25]

RISE OF ADIVASI MAHASABHA

The Adivasi Mahasabha was very much opposed to Congress politics and remained loyal to the British. Although we have discussed in preceding chapter how the inclusive politics of Gandhi did to a certain extent saw the involvement of a section of tribals in his mass movements over the 1920-43 periods but there was another section of Adivasis who was not interested in the bourgeois leadership of the Congress Party. This section of tribal leadership had raised the issue of separate statehood during the visit of Simon Commission in 1928 and Adivasi Mahasabha was the amalgamation of such leaders. It, therefore, remained outside the so-called mainstream nationalist politics. This was the reason why the party gained even the support of the Muslim League.

The second conference of Adivasi Mahasabha was held on 20 January 1939, where Jaipal Singh (*Marang Gomke* or the supreme leader), a Munda by birth, was elected as the President. Jaipal Singh was the son of a sarpanch of Takra village and was only 36 year old. He had studied in St. Paul's School, Ranchi, and later in 1919-20 he went to Darlington, England for pursuing higher studies. His allegiance to the

Anglican mission also inspired him to study at Augustine College, Canterbury. He was a brilliant hockey player and led the Indian hockey team to its golden trail in the 1928 Olympic Games. Jaipal Singh had a bright career and was also politically ambitious. On 21 January 1939, Jaipal delivered his first Presidential address and said,

"The Adivasi movement stands primarily for the moral and material advancement of Chota Nagpur and the Santhal Parganas, for the economic and political freedom of the aboriginal tracts and in sum, for the creation of a separate Governor's province comprising roughly Chota Nagpur and Santhal Parganas, with a government and administration appropriate to its needs. It is conceded everywhere that Chota Nagpur suffered by being tagged on to Bihar..... We have waited patiently and silently long enough for others to help us, we have trusted others in vain to help us march forward along the path of progress and improvement. Thank God, we have learnt our lesson in time. We must help ourselves. Our great future is in our own hands"[26]

The above-mentioned speech clearly demonstrates Jaipal Singh anti-Congress attitude. The worsening political situation in Chota Nagpur led the Congress Working Committee to entrust Dr. Rajendra Prasad to enquire into the causes of Adivasi unrest in Chota Nagpur and make a report on it. Prasad sought suggestions in redefined form to redress the Adivasis' grievances from Jaipal Singh for consideration and necessary steps.[27] Jaipal promptly submitted to him the demands of Adivasis which included: appointment of a Minister and a Parliamentary Secretary from the aboriginal communities on recommendation of the Adivasi Mahasabha; adequate representation of Adivasi in the government, legislature, services etc. in proportion to their numbers;

posting of officials well acquainted with the aboriginal's problems in the partially excluded areas; opening of a degree college at Ranchi; nomination of Adivasis to various committees and district boards etc.[28]

He impressed upon Rajendra Prasad that he too wanted Purna Swaraj and that the Adivasi Mahasabha was in full harmony with Gandhi's principles. He wanted Chota Nagpur and Santhal Parganas to be constituted into a Congress Province, separated and redeemed from Bihar and the question of a Governor's Province for Jharkhand to be studied and implemented from within the INC. He described his movement as thoroughly democratic and aimed at securing a place of honour in the national life of India.[29]

According to a secret West Bengal Police Report, when S.C. Bose visited Jamshedpur on 3 December 1939 to enlist support of the labourers against the war efforts of the British government, Jaipal Singh met Netaji and submitted an address on behalf of Adivasis demanding constitution of Chota Nagpur and Santhal Parganas into a separate Congress province. In December 1939 while addressing an Adivasi meeting presided over by Jaipal, Netaji advised the Adivasis to join Congress and capture the Congress machinery instead of nurturing hatred and separatism.[30]

Shortly after that Jaipal, busied himself in explaining to the Adivasis that the Congress government, which had already resigned, was the worst they could ever had. Jaipal Singh urged to form a separate state for the Adivasis and demanded a thorough investigation of the misdeeds of the Congress Ministry in Bihar. He supported the British in the Second World War and played a key role in recruiting tribals for the British army.[31]

Jaipal Singh planned an Adivasi rally at Ranchi duringthe Adivasi Mahasabha session to be held from 14 to 16 March 1940, a little before the 53rd session of INC going to be held on 19-20 March 1940 at Ramgarh under the Presidentship of Maulana Azad. Jaipal's anti-Congress attitude brought him closer to the Muslim League. The Muslim League, in the mid 1940's played with the idea of forming a corridor passing through the tribal areas to link the proposed areas which would constitute East and West Pakistan and thus gave financial support to the Adivasi Mahasabha. But when Jaipal witnessed the gruesome riots during the Direct Action Day, he realized the actual aim of the Muslim League and withdrew his support. He was not in favour of Pakistan and did not like to boycott the Assembly. He identified the land question as the most crucial and urged the speedy creation of a Jharkhand state. Simultaneously underlined was his commitment to the Indian Union when he raised the slogan of 'Jai Jharkhand! Jai Adivasi! Jai Hind!'[32] that combined local pride with a wider Indian patriotism. He even invited Nehru, Vijay Lakshmi Pandit and Jagjivan Ram to attend a meeting of Adivasi Mahasabha.[33]

THE CONSTITUTION MAKING AND ADIVASI MAHASABHA

Adivasi Mahasabha contested the elections of 1946 but could win only three seats in Bihar Assembly. Jaipal Singh was himself defeated by a Congress candidate Dr. P.C. Mitra. The nature of relationship between the Congress and the Adivasi Mahasabha can be gauged by the violence which erupted during the elections in 1946. In these elections fights broke out between them at various polling stations. In Khunti district, five Adivasis were killed and several injured in the violence, generating widespread condemnation. About this time Jaipal Singh was elected to the Constituent Assembly from Bihar on 23 July 1946.[34]

Jaipal Singh declared that Jharkhand was the land of the Adivasisand the non-Adivasis had exploited the Adivasis economically and politically; and there was little hope for their regeneration unless the intruders quit Jharkhand. During this period, Jaipal even preached violence to oust the intruders and achieve the goal of separate statehood. The educated Adivasi youth plunged into the movement against the non-Adivasis. Once Jaipal said to the Adivasis:

"Arise and wake up, recognize yourself, you all who had been toiling and sweating under the exploiting wolves for the last hundreds of years...get this firmly nailed down in your heads that you have not been destined to cut grass and draw water for the dikus all your lives. You have to take your place in the society on the basis of equality with others. So wake up, you are not inferior to anyone. Assert yourselves, and fight for your rights."

The demand for a separate state of Jharkhand was not new. Way back in January 1877, Colonel H.L. Thuillier, had prepared a map of Chotanagpur Division, in which were included the districts of Lohardaga, Hazaribagh, Manbhum and Singhbhum and the tributary states of Changbhakar, Korea, Surguja, Jashpur, Udaipur, Gangpur and Bonai.[35] The Adivasi Mahasabha had made this map the basis for its demand for an autonomous Chotanagpur state or a Jharkhand state.

In May 1947, the Adivasi Sabha of Jamshedpur wrote to Nehru, Gandhi and the Constituent Assembly urging the creation of Jharkhand state out of Bihar. 'We want Jharkhand Province to preserve and develop Adivasi culture and language', said their memorandum, 'to make our customary law supreme, to make our lands inalienable, and above all to save ourselves from continuous exploitation'.

The Constituent Assembly appointed a sub-committee headed by A.V.Thakkar to enquire into the tribal problems of the excluded and partially excluded areas (other than Assam) and recommend remedial measures to be suitably incorporated into the Constitution. Jaipal Singh and Phulbahan Saha were appointed its members. When the sub-committee visited Chota Nagpur in September 1947, the Adivasi Mahasabha and other tribal organizations submitted a memorandum demanding creation of Jharkhand Province.

Jaipal Singh held out hopes to his supporters that Jharkhand would soon be created, though he knew well that the sub-committee was not concerned with that. A.V.Thakkar wanted the constitutional safeguards to be provided to non-Christian tribals only, who were markedly less advanced than their Christian brethren. Jaipal Singh disagreed with him and ultimately no such provision could be incorporated in the constitution.

POST-INDEPENDENCE POLITICS AND CREATION OF JHARKHAND STATE

The exit of colonial masters, however, did not close the chapter of ethnic divide and regional separatism. Although the period under study is confined from 1858 to 1947 only but it shall not be out of context to give a passing reference to the politics of post-Independence era that finally capitalised in the merger of Chotanagpur and Santhal Parganas and the creation of Jharkhand state on 15th November 2000.

On 5 March 1949, the Adivasi Mahasabha held a conference of three thousand delegates at Hindisala in Ranchi and passed a resolution which declared that the Adivasi Mahasabha was being changed into the Jharkhand Party so as to fight for the formation of a separate Jharkhand state. In this conference, Jaipal Singh was elected as the President and Idsen Daba was elected as the Secretary.[36] Jaipal Singh soon had realized that to widen the support base of the movement for separate state, non-tribals also have to be brought into the fold. This point of view was stressed by Justin Richard who had earlier formed the United Jharkhand Bloc in 1948.[37]

The Jharkhand Party achieved remarkable success in the first general elections of 1951-52 winning 32 seats in the Bihar Assembly. As the second-largest party in the assembly, it secured the position of the main opposition party while the INC formed the government.[38]This electoral verdict seemed to give weight to the proposal of a new state of Jharkhand.

However, the States Reorganization Commission (SRC) rejected the proposal in its report on numerous grounds. Electorally, it cited the fact that the Jharkhand Party had failed to secure a clear majority in the concerned regions of the Chota Nagpur division and the Santhal Parganas in south Bihar.[39] Demographically, it mentioned that tribals made up of only one-third of the total population and the region consisted of several language groups, thereby making any decision in favour of Jharkhand a minority-based one. The Census of 1951 also showed that the tribals were not a very large community; in fact, they had never been a majority in the Chotanagpur region and the Census of 1941 had given an exaggerated figure of the tribal population in Chotanagpur. In 1951, the ST constituted 31.15 per cent of the population in Chota Nagpur and 44.67 per cent of the population in Santal Parganas. Thus, nearly two-thirds of Jharkhand's population was non-tribal.[40]Economically, the region provided an industrial balance to the agriculture-dominant plains in north Bihar as it contained coalfields, 40 per cent of India's mineral wealth, a steel plant at Jamshedpur, and Bihar's biggest thermal power plant at Bokaro, apart from a number of projects. The SRC recommended that a special development board, and not statehood, be considered for the region. It stated the arrangements set out in the Fifth schedule to the Constitution read with Scheduled Areas (Part 'A' States) to be fair and satisfactory.[41]

In 1963, the Jharkhand Party merged with the INC and left a temporary vacuum in the campaign for Jharkhand statehood. In 1972, the Jharkhand Mukti Morcha (JMM) was established by A.K. Roy (a Bengali- Marxist trade unionist), Shibu Soren (a Santhal tribal leader), and Binod Bihari Mahato (a Kurmi- Mahato leader). Through the 1970s and 1980s the JMM led the campaign for statehood while also pursuing a wider agenda of social activism that focussed on the marginalization of local people and the assertion of an Adivasi identity.[42] These included movements like the 'dhan katao andolan' (cut down paddy movement) and the 'jungle katao andolan' (cut down the forest movement) to protest against the state forestry policies. These activities helped develop the consciousness of a political Jharkhand as a precursor to a territorial Jharkhand.[43]

The success of the ethnic tribes in securing statehood in Nagaland (1963), Himachal Pradesh (1971) and Meghalaya,

Manipur and Tripura in 1972 and Mizoram and Arunachal Pradesh in 1987 have revealed that ethnic factors plus regionalism had strength to conquer. In Chotanagpur also the forces of internal colonialism and exploitation by better equipped population provided another incarnation for the separatist Jharkhand movement in the eighties.

Political developments aided the consolidation of this idea. In 1977, the Janata Party came to power both in the state and at the Centre. The new Bihar chief minister, Karpoori Thakur, reserved a proportion of the posts in government and educational institutions for Other Backward Castes (OBCs). The Janata Party nationally had been vocal about the need to reorganize state boundaries so as to correct economic imbalances and enable administrative convenience, even calling for a second States Reorganization Commission. However, while his national leadership was for it, the chief minister himself was opposed to the idea of Jharkhand. This resulted in a faction of party politicians rebelling. The rebel faction set up a 'Sangharsh Samiti' and passed a resolution in September 1977 calling for the establishment of a separate state of South Bihar.[44]

In 1980, the INC returned to power in Bihar and at the Centre. The Congress began to co-opt some of the JMM's platforms, and even agreed to a seat-sharing arrangement with Shibu Soren. This led to a formal split in the JMM by the end of 1984. By the late 1980s, the demand for Jharkhand had attracted the attention and support of a rising national party – the Bhartiya Janata Party (BJP). The BJP proposed the creation of Vananchal.

In July 1986, local activists of diverse backgrounds established the Jharkhand Coordination Committee (JCC) to change the statehood conversation to a cultural Jharkhandi identity issue rather than a minority tribal question. They presented a memorandum to the President of India in December 1987 demanding 21 districts from the four surrounding states of Bihar, M.P., Orissa and West Bengal. They pushed for statehood more aggressively, utilizing more direct-action methods like mass rallies, economic blockades and general strikes. As a result on 9 August 1995, the Jharkhand Area Autonomous Council was sworn in.[45]

In the meantime, the involvement of some of the JMM MP's including Shibu Soren, Suraj Mandal and others in a corruption case undermined their position. As a result the case of separate statehood appeared to loose force. But the BJP took up the cause and became very active on the demand of a separate state.

The BJP led National Democratic Alliance (NDA) came to power at the Centre after the 1999 Lok Sabha elections. The BJP had secured 11 out of 14 Lok Sabha seats of Jharkhand. As a result the NDA fulfilled its electoral promise of a separate State by passing the Bihar State Reorganization Bill 2000 from Lok Sabha on 2nd August 2000 and from Rajya Sabha on 11th August 2000. On 25th August 2000, the then President K.R. Narayan gave his approval on the bill and consequently Jharkhand became the 28th state of India on 15th November 2000.Prabhat Kumar became the first Governor of Jharkhand and Babulal Marandi the first Chief Minister of the state.

Therefore, the state of Jharkhand was formed after a century of continued protests and movements spearheaded by the ethnic tribes in Chotanagpur. The protest movement and agitation of indigenous autochthones was against imperialism and colonialism, both internal and external. The focus on ethnic differences, racial and religious divide, and regional chasms were developed by the colonial rulers with two fold purpose of underscoring the economic exploitation and setting the stage for paternalism as a shield and succour for the victims by the victors.[46]The point has been succinctly made by Devalle in his study in the following words:

"It was precisely at the moment of colonial conquest that the indigenous and ethnic problematiques emerged in the non-western world as social phenomena with specific characteristics. These problematiques are, in origin, aspects of the colonial expansion in which racism and the fostering of ethnic differences formed part of the strategy for domination."[47]

Therefore, we saw in this chapter how the sense of tribal identity and political slogan of a separate state shifted the emphasis of the government to the conditions of the tribals, the nature and consequences of exploitation, isolation and neglect. The old colonial policy of paternalism, i.e. putting the tribes in scheduled category and recurrent amendments in the constitution extending their reservation, amendment of land laws for restoration of all tribal lands (Bihar Act, 1969), emphasis on special development of area (Chotanagpur and Santal Parganas Development Authority, 1972) and exploitation of mines and forests through grandiose industrial projects leading to dispossession of tribal lands and large scale outsiders' immigration, and emigration of tribes due to famines and resultant decay in tribal population, the acceleration in conversions and the Church beholden to the rulers, all seem to be a continuation of the features of the earlier colonialism and strategy of domination.[48]There was a better articulated demand for a dominant role for the tribals in regional administration, for better educational facilities, and more employment opportunities.[49] There was also a demand for restoration of alienated land provision for legal and institutional safeguards to protect tribal interests and to end all forms of exploitation.[50] All parties working in Chotanagpur united in stressing the regional factor.

NOTES AND REFERENCES

1. De, Debasree. *Gandhi and Adivasis*, New Delhi, 2022, p 132.

2. Singh, K.S. *Tribal Movements in India*, vol. II, Manohar Publishers: New Delhi, 2006, pp.1-2.

3. Notable works of Sarat Chandra Roy are '*The Mundas and Their Country*', Ranchi, 1912; '*The Oraons of Chota Nagpur*', Ranchi, 1915; and '*The Birhors, a Little Known Jungle Tribe of Chota Nagpur*', Ranchi, 1925.

4. De, Debasree, op. cit., p. 133.

5. Peter Tete, S.J. *A Missionary Social Worker in India*, Roma, 1984, p.93.

6. Chatterji, P.C. (ed.) *Self-images, Identity and Nationality*, Indian Institute of Advanced Study, Shimla, p.155.

7. Singh, S.K. *Inside Jharkhand*, Ranchi, 2006, pp. 63-64.

8. Das, Victor. *Jharkhand: Castle over the Graves*, Inter-India Publications, New Delhi, 1944, p.90.

9. Jha, A.K. *Dreams and Dilemma: Jharkhand Movement*, Syndicate, 1996, p.50.

10. Editorial, *The Search Light*, December 16, 1930.

11. De, Debasree, op. cit. pp. 92-93.

12. Rana, L.N. "Introduction of Provincial Autonomy (1937-39) and the Jharkhand region of Bihar." *Proceedings of the Indian History Congress*, vol. 58, 1997, pp.519-29.

13. Bharathi, K.S. *Encyclopaedia of Eminent Thinkers: The Political thought of Jawaharlal Nehru*, vol.2, 1998, New Delhi, pp.70-96.

14. Choudhary, R.K. "Government of India Act, 1935 and the Congress in Power (1935-39)" in P.N. Ojha (ed.) *History of Indian National Congress in Bihar*, KPJRI, Patna, 1985, p.449.

15. Rana, L.N. op. cit. pp.520.

16. Ibid, pp.521-523.

17. Diwakar, R.R. *Bihar through the Ages*, Calcutta: Orient Longmans, 1959, pp. 663-664.

18. Rana, L.N. op. cit. p.524.

19. Kumar, Nirdosh. *The Making of Adivasi Mahasabha*, Lucknow, 2019, p.62.

20. Ibid, p.100.

21. Ibid, p.101.

22. Fortnightly confidential report from Bihar and Orissa for the second half of January 1935, Patna dated 1st February 1935. Home Political File No. 18/1/1935 cited in A.K. Chattoraj, "Political Factors behind Separatism and the Formation of Jharkhand Party", *Proceedings of the Indian History Congress*, vol. 61 (2000-01), pp. 1038-1042.

23. Singh, K.S. op. cit. pp.4-5.

24. Rana, L.N. op. cit. pp.525-526.

25. Diwakar, R.R. op. cit. p. 664.

26. The first public speech of Jaipal Singh in Adivasi Mahasabha Rally on 20th January 1939, Ranchi cited in A.K. Pankaj (ed.) *"Adivasidom: Selected Writings and Speeches of Jaipal Singh Munda"*, Ranchi, 2017, pp. 105-109.

27. Rajendra Prasad to Jaipal Singh, 18 May 1939; Valmiki Choudhary, ed. *Dr. Rajendra Prasad: Correspondenceand Select Documents*, New Delhi: Allied Publishers, vol. III, 1984, p.82.

28. Jaipal Singh to Rajendra Prasad, 24 May and 14 June 1939, ibid, pp.97, 128.

29. *The Bihar Herald*, 27 June 1939, p.14.

30. Sinha, S.P.*Conflict and Tension in Tribal Society*, New Delhi, 1993, p. 288.

31. This change in the attitude of Jaipal Singh could be observed from his articles that were published in *The Bihar Herald*, 4 July 1939, p.17 and *The Sentinel*, 2 June 1940, Ranchi.

32. He started his presidential speech to All India Adivasi Mahasabha at Ranchi on 28 Feb 1948 with this salutation.

33. Sinha, S.P. op. cit. p.292.

34. Rana, L.N. "The Adivasi Mahasabha (1938-1949): Launching Pad of the Jharkhand Movement", *Proceedings of theIndian History Congress,* vol. 53 (1992), pp.397-405.

35. See Appendix

36. Mahapatra, L.K. "The Jharkhand Party in Orissa" in K.S. Singh (ed.) *Tribal Movements in India*, vol. II, Manohar Publishers, New Delhi, 1983, p.67.

37. Sachidananda, B. "The Tribal Situation in Bihar" in K.S. Singh (ed.) *Tribal Situation in India*, Indian Institute of Advanced Study, Shimla, 1972, p.175.

38. Chandra, B., Mukherjee, M. and Mukherjee, A.*India After Independence 1947-2000*, Penguin Publications, New Delhi,2002, p.117.

39. *Report of the States Reorganisation Commission*, 1955, p.169.

40. Chandra, B., Mukherjee, M. and Mukherjee, A. op. cit. p.116.

41. *Report of the States Reorganisation Commission*, 1955, p.170.

42. Srinivasan, V.S. *The Origin Story of India's States* (e-book), Penguin Random House India, 2021, pp.41-42.

43. Tillin, Louise. *Remapping India: New States and Their Political Origins*, New Delhi: Oxford University Press, 2013, pp. 75-76.

44. Meena, K.P. *Adivasi Vidroh*, Anugya Books: New Delhi, 2021, pp.105-108.

45. Srinivasan, V.S. op. cit. 66-68.

46. Sharma, A.P. "Colonial Dimensions of Regionalism: A Case Study of Jharkhand Movement", *Proceedings of the Indian History Congress*, vol. 53 (1992), pp. 351-366.

47. Devalle, B.C. Susana. *Discourses of Ethnicity: Culture and Protest in Jharkhand*, Sage Publication, 1992, pp. 14-15.

48. Sharma, A.P. op. cit. pp. 351-366.

49. Mahato, P.P. "Assertion and Reassertion as Jharkhandi: A History of the Indigenous People 1763-2007", in Asha Mishra and C.K. Paty (ed.) Tribal Movements in Jharkhand 1857-2007, Concept Publishing Company, New Delhi, 2010, p. 55

50. Singh, K.S. op. cit. p.9.

CONCLUSION

The British intrusion in the plateau of Chotanagpur took place after the grant of Diwani of Bengal, Bihar and Orissa to the East India Company by Mughal Emperor Shah Alam II in 1765. As they expanded their control in the hills and forests of Chotanagpur plateau, stretching from Birbhum and Manbhum to Central India and from the fort of Rohtasgarh in Shahabad to borders of Orissa, they came in contact with the non-Aryan tribes who were never completely subjugated till the advent of the British and had retained their tribal organisation, religion, customs and language so far.

Like the rest of the country, Chotanagpur was brought under the formal and rigid canopy of state power. The British imposed their administration, revenue laws and judicial system that deranged the placidity of the tribal life, customs and traditions of communal ownership of land. Resistance, rebellions and protests were the inevitable results as even the Rajas or feudal chiefs found it difficult to meet the growing revenue demands of the British rulers. The tribal conflicts in the Company era (1865-1857), was a 'phase of primary resistance' resulting from the infiltration of non-tribals into tribal territory, have been interpreted as the resistance of tribals against exploitative alien outsiders, the dikus, whose influx into the tribal region increased with the new economic opportunities ushered in by British rule.

Tamar rebellion of 1819-20, Kol Rebellion of 1831-32, Bhumij Revolt of 1832-33 and the Santhal Hul of 1855-57, for instance, were traced to primarily four causes – rapacious moneylenders, the increasing misery caused by the system of personal and hereditary bondage for debt, corruption and extortions of the police and the impossibility of the tribals obtaining redress in the courts. However these early uprisings were in fact not against the Government, but mainly against the local Rajas and the Zamindars. But as the British wanted to consolidate their power in Chotanagpur, they had to interfere and they naturally sided with the local Rajas and landlords because they were influential people and their cooperation would have proved quite beneficial for the alien rulers. It was much due to the British power that all these rebellions which occurred in Chotanagpur before the outbreak of the Revolt of 1857 were crushed with iron hands.

In the backdrop of these revolts and rebellions, some administrative, political and socio-economic reforms were also carried out from time to time. Under Regulation XIII of 1833 (after the Kol rebellion) and Act XXXVII of 1855 (after the Santal Hul) for instance, special rules were framed for the area which eased conflicts within tribal society. In 1834, Southwest Frontier Agency with its headquarters in Kishanpur (Ranchi) was established. This brought the whole region under effective control of the British rule. In 1854, the designation of the South-West Frontier Agency was changed to Chotanagpur division,and was composed of five districts – Hazaribagh, Ranchi, Palamau, Manbhum and Singhbhum. This was administered as a non-regulation province under a Commissioner reporting to the Lieutenant Governor of Bengal.

The post-1857 period and the takeover of the administration directly by the Crown gave the necessary government patronage to the Christian missionaries who worked in Chotanagpur and saw here a fertile field for evangelisation. The aborigines were lured by material and educational benefits of the Churches that opened hospitals, schools and other charitable institutions. The missionaries found the land issue to be an ideal instrument for attracting the tribals to their fold and took up the cases of tribals and raised slogans for the restoration of all lands to the tribals, and freedom from impositions like Beth-begari and other praedial conditions.This led to the flocking of the tribals to the Church and the number of converts started growing tremendously as the missionaries took up their cases and helped in litigations that soon developed into the Sardar movement.

The Sardari Larai was the first serious challenge to the concept of landlord property, which was at the basis of the Permanent Settlement. The Sardars or the Christian converts adopted peaceful means like prayers, petition and protest to demand justice from colonial regime against landlords' beth-begari (labour demands) and encroachments on bhuinhari lands; the Sardars demanded that they pay rent directly to the Government. Although the movement started in the year 1858, it only gained momentum after the failure of Chotanagpur Tenure Act (1869) and operations following on it – the Bhuinhari survey and the Settlement operation as they failed to restore the ancestral land rights of the tribes.

Another movement of the nineteenth century which had agrarian discontent as its root cause was the Kherwar movement of the Santal tribes in Chotanagpur. It was an agrarian issue and not religious one because the demands of Santals included the restoration of their land, opposition to enhancing rent and census operations and encroachment to their grazing land and forest wealth, although they made use of the religious myths, legends and superstitions for uniting the people to launch struggle for their economic betterment. The movement however soon ended as its leaders Bhagirath and Dubia Gosain were prosecuted by the government.

Another common theme that we saw was the role of the 'rebellious prophets' who launched 'messianic movements', promising their followers to drive out the outsiders and bring back a golden age. Once the 'lost kingdom' was recovered, 'there will be enough to eat, no famine, the people will live together in harmony.' This was a millenarian goal. The Ulgulan movement and the Sapha Ho movement illustrate two crucial elements of millenarianism: appearance of a charismatic leader as the exponent of its radical ideology, and the pervasive belief among the rebels that their cause would inevitably triumph because it has been blessed by a supernatural agency.

Another concept in connection with such movements is that of religious revitalization and cultural purification. The aim of these movements was either a complete religious reformation or a renaissance and a restoration of the old religious beliefs. The leadership came from religious leaders like Birsa Munda who claimed to be the incarnations of God, and asserted that they had received messages from supernatural powers and was divinely ordained, and therefore, infallible.

Birsa's Ulgulan also had a tinge of proto-nationalism or anti-colonial utopia. This conception is based on the fact that Birsa's 'real enemies [were] the saheblok [white folk] and the Government. He sought to establish a sort of 'monastic governmentality.' From the historical standpoint Birsa and his followers have attained the status of martyrs and even today in folk songs and anecdotes their memory lingers. Therefore, the second phase of tribal movements in Chotanagpur (1858-1917) thus saw a curious mix of agrarian, religious and political issues.

The third phase of tribal movement (1917-1938) saw the rise of the tribal movements of a secular or political nature. After the death of Birsa Munda, his movement virtually came to an end. But Birsa and his followers had prepared the soil for a greater national movement under the leadership of Mahatma Gandhi. The tribal movements in the Gandhian era such as the Tana Bhagat movement in the 1920s and the Hari Baba movement of early 1930s though were cultural revitalization movements in nature but were caused by the rise of political radicalism in the wake of Gandhian Non-Cooperation movement. The Adivasis were constantly supporting Gandhian ideology of non-violence, non-payment of taxation, idioms of purity, temperance and vegetarianism, constructive programmes like khadi and charkha. Now they had a millenarian dream of establishing Swaraj or Gandhi Raj.

At another level, the Gandhian constructive programmes initiated the process of politicization of the Adivasis, nurtured a generation of Adivasi leaders, and provided a common platform for both Adivasis and non-Adivasis, thus bringing the first into the mainstream of national politics. A large number of tribals joined the Gandhian movement and participated both in combative and constructive programmes launched by Gandhi.

Under the banner of Gandhi, the tribals also found a suitable path to attack the forest regulations which had curtailed the customary rights of tribals in forests. 'Forest Satyagraha' – the reassertion by poor peasants and tribals of traditional customary rights over forests 'reserved' by the colonial state – represents an almost forgotten but fascinating aspect of Gandhian era. With the help of Congress, Forest Satyagraha was organised by the Hos under the leadership of Harihar Mahto.

The fourth phase of tribal movements in Chotanagpur (1938-1947) saw the emergence of a new wave of regionalism based on tribes' security against outsiders. The Government of India Act of 1935 put Chotanagpur in the category of 'partially excluded areas' under a special responsibility of Governor. After the Provincial elections in 1937 and the rout of the regional political parties in Chotanagpur at the hands of the Congress, there was another call for pan-tribal unity as Adivasi Mahasabha was formed in 1938.

Jaipal Singh, an Oxford educated Christian tribal leader took the reins of the Mahasabha in 1939 demanding complete separation of Chotanagpur from Bihar. It followed a British loyalist and anti-nationalist path during the Second World War, and Muslim League also provided it financial help with the vision of creating Chotanagpur as a corridor between East and West Pakistan. But after the defeat in the elections of 1946, the Mahasabha parted its ways with the Muslim League and agreed to join the mainstream of nationalist and constitutional politics.

The dawn of independence in 1947 and the exit of colonial masters, however, did not close the chapter of ethnic divide and regional separatism. The Adivasi Mahasabha shed its ethnic nomenclature and adopted a regional nomenclature in its new incarnation as the Jharkhand Party (1950). The result was that ethnicity and regional separatism now crystallised into the demand for a Jharkhand state carved out of the tribal territories. The new experiment brought rich dividends as the party won 33 seats in the elections of 1951-52 and became the main opposition party in the Bihar Assembly.

A jolt was received soon as the State Reorganisation Commission in its report in 1955 rejected their demand as the Jharkhand tribes lacked linguistic homogeneity and took away certain portions of Chotanagpur and added them to West Bengal thus further corroding the regional base. The subsequent elections in 1957 and 1962 led to the decay in the fortunes of the party and the party committed a tactical mistake by merging with the Congress in 1963 that gave it a death blow.

Subsequent developments however, belied the hope. The success of ethnic tribes in securing statehood in Nagaland (1963), Himachal Pradesh (1971), Meghalaya, Manipur and Tripura (1972) and Mizoram and Arunachal Pradesh in 1987 had revealed that ethnic factors plus regionalism had strength to conquer. Finally the demand was accepted by the NDA government and the Bihar State Reorganization Bill 2000 was passed from Lok Sabha on 2nd August 2000 and from Rajya Sabha on 11th August 2000. On 25th August 2000, the then President K.R. Narayan gave his approval on the bill and consequently Jharkhand became the 28th state of India on 15th November 2000.

Therefore this research have tried to challenge the contour of homogenous nature of tribal movements presented by the erstwhile scholars. There was a marked transition in the nature of tribal movements in Chotanagpur from a phase of primary resistance in the first half of nineteenth century to a phase of organised petition movement against agrarian and forest acts in the second half of nineteenth century. The genesis, growth and direction of these tribal movements were directly conditioned and regulated by the leadership pattern and the structure of movement-bearing society. For instance we saw how there was a shift from religious movements and millenarianism under Birsa and Bhagirath to political movements and nationalism under Gandhi and finally regionalism under Jaipal Munda.

APPENDIX I

Renell's Map of Chota Nagpur. Possibly 1780's vintage

© National Archive of

APPENDIX II

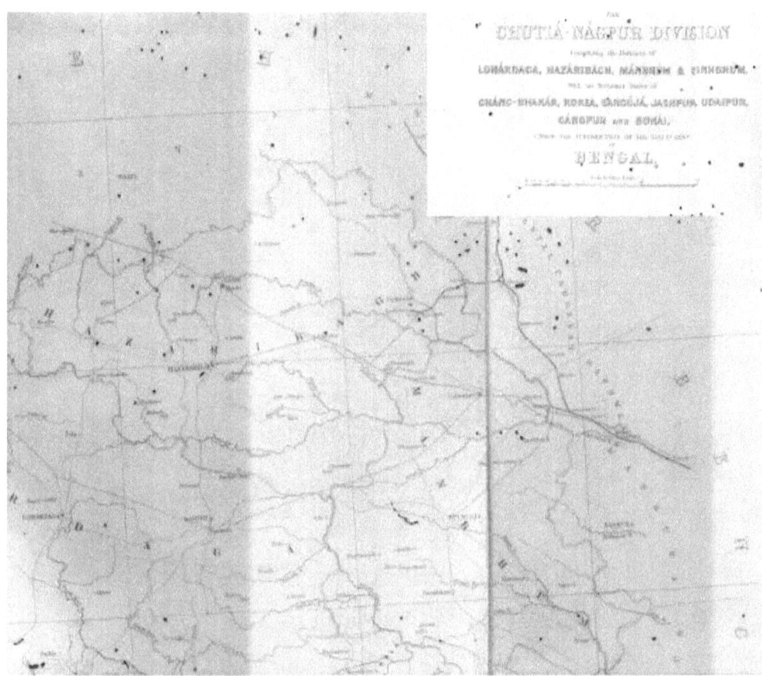

Chota Nagpur Division. Published in 1877 under the direction of Col H.L. Thuillier. (Extract of the original map shown here). The map was specially published for the statistical Account of Bengal by W.W. Hunter.

APPENDIX III

**'Founding members and leaders of the
Adivasi Mahasabha in 1939'**

[**1st Row Sitting:** 1st person- not known, 2nd- Theble Oraon, 3rd- Theodore Surin, 4th- Jaipal Singh, 5th- Rai sahib Bandi Ram Oraon, 6th- Paul Dayal, 7th- Nehemiah Kujur.

2nd Row Sitting:1st- Ignes Beck, 2nd- not known, 3rd- not known.

3rd Row Standing: 1st- not known, 2nd- Mr. Amin, 3rd- Boniface Lakra, 4th- Julius Tigga, 5th- not known, 6th- Michel Tigga, 7th- Harman Lakra.

4th Row Standing: 1st- not known, 2nd- Dayal Kujur, 3rd- not known.]

(Source- Munda, R.D. and Mullick S.B. *The Jharkhand Movement: Indigenous Peoples' Struggle for Autonomy in India,* Copenhagen, 2003,p.15)

APPENDIX IV

JHARKHAND RESOLUTION OF ADIVASI MAHASABHA

"Whereas it is recognised that Jharkhand, i.e. the Aboriginal Tracts commonly known as Chotanagpur Division and the District of Santhal Parganas, is in respect of area, size and population large enough to become a separate, compact and autonomous administrative unit;

Whereas the present arrangement, whereby the legislature is constituted of two elements with not much in common between them, is hostile to aboriginal development;

Whereas the moral, material and the cultural progress of the said Aboriginal Tracts can never be secured under the existing arrangements, and whereas the creation of separate Governor's province comprising the said Aboriginal Tracts is vital for the peace and good Government of Jharkhand;

This conference which is representative of all sections of people of the Chotanagpur plateau demands the immediate creation of Jharkhand province comprising the Adivasi tracts, together with any adjacent areas, such as the states of Seraikela, Kharsawan, Keonjhar, Bonai, Bamra, Surguja, Udaipur, Korea and Gangpur, Jashpur and Changbhakar, which are historically, geographically, ethnically, culturally and administratively part and parcel of the Chotanagpur Plateau, which can be conveniently included."

(The *Jharkhand Resolution* passed at 2nd Annual Session of the Adivasi Mahasabha in 1939)

BIBLIOGRAPHY

PRIMARY SOURCES

1. Abul Fazl, *Akbarnama* (tr. Beveridge), vol. III, Asiatic Society: Calcutta, 2000.

2. Afif, *Tarikh-i-Firoz Shahi*, tr. Wilayat Husain, Calcutta, 1890.

3. Bradley-Birt, F.B. '*Chota Nagpur: A Little- known Province of the Empire*', London, 1910.

4. Hunter, W.W. '*Annals of Rural Bengal*', New York, 1868.

5. Hunter, W.W. '*Statistical Account of Bengal*', vol. XVII, London, 1877.

6. Hunter, W.W. *Bengal Ms. Records*, Vol. I, London, 1894.

7. Jahangir. *Tuzuk-i-Jahangiri* (translated by Rogers, A.) (Edited by Beveridge H.), vol. I, Munshiram Manoharlal: Delhi, 1968.

8. Mirza Nathan, *Baharistan-i-Ghaybi* (tr. Borah), vol. I, Assam, 1936.

9. Reid, J. *Final Report on the Survey and Settlement Operations in the District of Ranchi 1902-1910*, Calcutta, 1912.

10. Renny, R.H. 'Report on the Census of the District Singhbhum 1891.'

11. *Report of the States Reorganisation Commission*, 1955.

12. Revenue Proceedings (Land Revenue, Agriculture and Forest), Government of Bengal, Bihar and Orissa

13. Sachau, *Alberuni's India*, Vol. II, London, 1910.

14. Shah Nawaz Khan & Abdul Hayy, *Maathir-ul-Umara* (tr. Beveridge), vol. II, Calcutta Oriental Press Ltd.: Calcutta, 1952.

GAZETTEERS

1. Hunter, W.W. 'The Imperial Gazetteer of India', vol. XXIII, Oxford, 1908.

2. Kumar, N. *Bihar District Gazetteers: Ranchi*, Patna, 1970.

3. Lister, E. *District Gazetteer of Hazaribagh*, Patna, 1917.

4. Macpherson, T.S. and Hallett, M.G. '*Bihar and Orissa District Gazetteers: Ranchi*', Patna, 1917.

5. O' Malley, L.S.S. '*Bengal District Gazetteers: Singhbhum, Seraikela and Kharsawan*', Bengal Secretariat Book Depot: Calcutta, 1910.

6. Roy Chaudhuri, P.C. *Bihar District Gazetteers: Singhbhum*, Patna, 1958.

SECONDARY SOURCES

Books

1. Anderson P.B. "Revival, Syncretism and the Anticolonial Discourse of the Kherwar Movement, 1871-1910", in Young, R.F. (ed.) *India and the Indianness of Christianity*, Eerdmans Publishing Co., U.S.A, 2009.

2. Ansari, T.H. *Mughal Administration and the Zamindars of Bihar*, 2019.

3. Areeparampil, M. *Struggle for Swaraj*, TRTC, Chaibasa, 2002.

4. Areeparampil, Mathew. 'Socio-cultural and Religious Movements among the Ho Tribals of Singhbhum District of Bihar', in *Continuity and Change in Tribal Society*, ed. Mrinai Miri, Shimla: Indian Institute of Advanced Studies, 1993.

5. Bharathi, K.S. *Encyclopaedia of Eminent Thinkers: The Political thought of Jawaharlal Nehru*, vol.2, 1998, New Delhi.

6. Bhuyan, A.C. *The Quit India Movement*, Manas Publications: New Delhi, 1975.

7. Bose, N.K. The Structure of Hindu Society.

8. Chandra, B., Mukherjee, M. and Mukherjee, A. *India after Independence 1947-2000*, Penguin Publications, New Delhi, 2002.

9. Chatterji, P.C. (ed.) *Self-images, Identity and Nationality*, Indian Institute of Advanced Study, Shimla.

10. Chaudhary, Prasanna Kumar and Srikant. *Bihar-Jharkhand me Mahayuddha* (in Hindi), Patna, 2008.

11. Chaudhary, Prasanna Kumar and Srikant. *Bihar-Jharkhand me Mahayuddha* (in Hindi), Patna, 2008.

12. Chaudhury, Buddhadeb (ed.) *Tribal Transformation in India,* vol. III in Tribal Studies of India Series, New Delhi: Inter India Publications, 1992.

13. Chopra, P.N. *Quit India Movement*, Publications Division, Govt. of India, New Delhi, 1987.

14. Choudhary, Valmiki (ed.) *Dr. Rajendra Prasad: Correspondence and Select Documents*, New Delhi: Allied Publishers, vol. III, 1984.

15. Coupland, R. *India, A Restatement.*

16. Das, Victor. *Jharkhand: Castle over the Graves*, Inter-India Publications, New Delhi, 1944.

17. Datta, K.K '*History of the Freedom Movement in Bihar*' in 3 vols. Patna, 1957.

18. Datta, K.K. '*Santal Insurrection*', Calcutta, 1940.

19. Datta, K.K. *Bengal Subah*, Vol. I.

20. Datta, K.K. *Writings and Speeches of Gandhiji Relating to Bihar from 1927 to 1947*, Govt. of Bihar, Patna, March 1967.

21. De Sa, Fidelis. *Crisis in Chotanagpur*, Redenptorist Publications: Bangalore, 1975.

22. De, Debasree. *Gandhi and Adivasis*, New Delhi, 2022.

23. Devalle, B.C. Susana. *Discourses of Ethnicity: Culture and Protest in Jharkhand*, Sage Publication, 1992.

24. Dhan, A.K. *Birsa Munda,* Publication Division: New Delhi, (kindle edition).

25. Diwakar, R.R. *Bihar through the Ages*, Calcutta: Orient Longmans, 1959.

26. Dutta, K.K. *Anti- British Plots and Movements*, Meenakshi Prakashan: Mccrut, 2006.

27. Elwin, Verrier '*The Kol Insurrection*', Man in India, vol. XXV (4), 1945

28. Fuchs, Stephen '*Rebellious Prophets*', Delhi, 1980.

29. Goswami, P. *Untold Story of Chota Nagpur: Its journey with the Colonial Army 1767-1947*, Chennai, 2020.

30. Gupta, Ramnika (ed.) *Adivasi Shaurya evam Vidroh (Jharkhand)*, Surbhi Publishers: Delhi, 2015.

31. Gupta, S.D. *'Peasant and Tribal Movements in Colonial Bengal: A Historiographic Overview'* in Sekhar Bandyopadhyay ed. *'Bengal: Rethinking History'*.

32. Gupta, S.D. *Adivasis and the Raj: Socio- Economic Transition of the Hos 1820-1932*, Orient Blackswan, New Delhi, 2011.

33. Hodne, Olav. *"L.O. Skrefsrud, Missionary and Social Reformer among the Santals of Santal Parganas: With Special Reference to the Periods between 1867 and 1881"*, Oslo, 1966.

34. Hoffmann, J.B. Encyclopaedia Mundarika, 1932, vol. V.

35. Jha, A.K. *Dreams and Dilemma: Jharkhand Movement*, Syndicate, 1996.

36. Jha, J.C. *'The Bhumij Revolt (1832-33)'*

37. Jha, J.C. *'The Kol Insurrection of Chota-Nagpur'*, Calcutta, 1964.

38. Jha, J.C. *The Indian National Congress and the Tribals*, New Delhi, 1985.

39. Kumar, Nirdosh. *The Making of Adivasi Mahasabha*, Lucknow, 2019.

40. Lal Pradumn Singh. *'Nagvansh'*, Lucknow, 1951, part II.

41. MacDougall, John *'Land or Religion? The Sardar and Kherwar Movements in Bihar 1858-95'*, New Delhi, 1985.

42. Mahto, S. *'Hundred Years of Christian Missions in Chotanagpur since 1845'*, Ranchi, 1971.

43. Mathur, L.P. *'Tribal Revolts in India under British Raj'*, Jaipur, 2004

44. Meena, K.P. *Adivasi Vidroh*, Anugya Books: New Delhi, 2021.

45. Mishra, Asha and Paty, C.K. (ed.) Tribal Movements in Jharkhand 1857-2007, Concept Publishing Company, New Delhi, 2010.

46. Mishra, S. *"History of the Freedom Movement in Chotanagpur"*, Patna, 1990.

47. Munda, R.D. and Mullick S.B. *The Jharkhand Movement: Indigenous Peoples' Struggle for Autonomy in India*, Copenhagen, 2003.

48. O' Malley, L.S.S. *History of Bengal, Bihar and Orissa under British Rule*, Calcutta, 1925.

49. Ojha, P.N. (ed.) *History of Indian National Congress in Bihar*, KPJRI, Patna, 1985.

50. Pandey, S.K. *History and Culture of Jharkhand*, Agra, 2020.

51. Pankaj, A.K. (ed.) *"Adivasidom: Selected Writings and Speeches of Jaipal Singh Munda"*, Ranchi, 2017.

52. Peter Tete, S.J. *A Missionary Social Worker in India: J.B. Hoffmann, the Chota Nagpur Tenancy Act and the Catholic Cooperatives 1893-1928*, Roma, 1984.

53. Qanungo, K.R. *Shershah and His Times*, 1965, p. 181.

54. Raghavaiah, V. *'Tribal Revolts'*, Nellore, 1971.

55. Roy Chaudhary, P.C. *Bihar mein 1857*.

56. Roy, S.C. '*The Birhors, a Little Known Jungle Tribe of Chota Nagpur*', 1925.

57. Roy, S.C. '*The Mundas and Their Country*', Ranchi, 1912.

58. Roy, S.C. '*The Oraons of Chota Nagpur*', Ranchi, 1915.

59. Singh, K.S. (ed.) *Tribal Situation in India*, Shimla: Indian Institute of Advanced Studies, 1972.

60. Singh, K.S. 'Haribaba and his Movement: Changes in Chota Nagpur', *Tribal Transformation in India,* vol. III in Tribal Studies of India Series, ed. Buddhadeb Chaudhury, New Delhi: Inter India Publications, 1992.

61. Singh, K.S. '*The Dust Storm and the Hanging Mist: A study of Birsa Munda and his movement in Chotanagpur, 1874-1901*', Calcutta, 1966.

62. Singh, K.S. '*Tribal Movement in India*', in 3 vols. Delhi, 1982.

63. Singh, K.S. *Birsa Munda and His Movement 1874-1901: A study of a Millenarian Movement in Chotanagpur*, Oxford University Press: Calcutta, 1983.

64. Singh, Lata. *Popular Translations of Nationalism Bihar, 1920-1922*, New Delhi, 2012.

65. Singh, S.K. *Inside Jharkhand*, Ranchi, 2006.

66. Sinha, B.B. *Socio- Economic Life in Chotanagpur 1858-1935*, B.R. Publishing: Delhi, 1979.

67. Sinha, S.P. *Conflict and Tension in Tribal Society*, New Delhi, 1993.

68. Sinha, S.P. *Life and Times of Birsa Bhagwan*, Ranchi, 1964.

69. Sinha, Sudha. *The Nagvanshis of Chotanagpur*, New Delhi, 2001.

70. Sitaramayya, P. *History of Indian National Congress*, vol. II (1935-1947), New Delhi: S. Chand, 1969.

71. Slim, W.J. *Defeat into Victory: Battling Japan in Burma and India 1942-1945*, Natraj Publishers: Dehra Dun, 1981.

72. Srinivasan, V.S. *The Origin Story of India's States* (e-book), Penguin Random House India, 2021.

73. Srivastava, A.R.N. '*Tribal Freedom Fighters of India*', New Delhi, 2009.

74. Thornton, E. *The History of the British Empire in India*, vol. V, London, 1841-43.

75. Tillin, Louise. *Remapping India: New States and Their Political Origins*, New Delhi: Oxford University Press, 2013.

76. Verma, R.C. '*Indian Tribes through the Ages*', New Delhi.

77. Vidyarthi, L.P., Srivastava, B.R. and Sahay, B.N., *Gandhi and Social Sciences*, New Delhi, Book Hive, 1970.

78. Virottam, B. *Jharkhand: Itihaas evam Sanskriti*' (in Hindi), Patna, 2001.

79. Virottam, Balmukund. *The Nagbanshis and the Cheros*, New Delhi, 1972.

80. Winternitz. *A History of Indian Literature*, Vol. II, Calcutta, 1933.

Articles/ Journals

1. Banerji, Man Gobinda. "The Name Chota Nagpur", *Journal of the Bihar and Orissa Research Society*, Vol. XXVI, 1940, pp.189-223.

2. Blockmann, H. "Notes from Mohammadan Historians on Chutia Nagpur, Pachet and Palamau", *JASB*, 1871

3. Chattoraj, A.K. "Political Factors behind Separatism and the Formation of Jharkhand Party", *Proceedings of the Indian History Congress*, vol. 61 (2000-01), pp. 1038-1042.

4. Damodaran, Vinita. "Environment, Ethnicity and History of Chotanagpur, India, 1850-1970", *Environment and History*, Vol.3, No.3, 1997.

5. Dhan, R.O. 'The Problems of the Tana Bhagats of Ranchi District', *Bulletin of Bihar Tribal Welfare Research Institute*, Ranchi, vol. 2, 1960, p.169.

6. Gautam, Ambrish. "Chota Nagpur- An Untold History: A Socio-Historical Analysis", *Anthropology*, Vol.5, 2017, pp.1-18.

7. Ghosh, A. "Jharkhand Movement in West Bengal", *Economic and Political Weekly*, vol. 28, Jan. 1993, pp. 121-127.

8. Gupta, S.D. "Accessing Nature: Agrarian Change, Forest Laws and their Impact on an Adivasi Economy in Colonial India", *Conservation and Society*, 7(4), 2009, pp. 227-238.

9. Jha, A.P. "Nature of the Santhal Unrest of 1871-1875 and Origin of the Sapha Hor Movement", *Indian Historical*

Records Commission (Proceedings) 35, pt. 2 (1960), pp. 103-113.

10. Jha, J.C. "The Kol Rising of Chotanagpur (1831-33): Its Causes", *Proceedings of Indian History Congress*, vol. 21 (1958), pp. 440-446.

11. Kumar, Anil. "An Unknown Chapter of Kol-Insurrection", Proceedings of Indian History Congress, vol. 62(2001), pp. 621-626.

12. Kumar, Sanjay. "The Civil Disobedience Movement and the Tribes of Bihar (1930-33)", *JASRAE*, Vol. XII, Issue no. 23, Oct 2016, pp.544-548.

13. Kumar, Sanjay. "The Civil Disobedience Movement and the Tribes of Bihar (1930-33)", *JASRAE*, Vol. XII, Issue no. 23, Oct 2016, pp.544-548.

14. MacDougall, John. "Agrarian reform vs. Religious revitalization: Collective Resistance to Peasantization among the Mundas, Oraons, and Santals, 1858-95", *Contributions to Indian Sociology*, vol. 11, no.2 (1977), pp. 295-321.

15. Mallick, Ata. *Encroachment on the Rights of the Adivasis: Colonial Forest Policy in 19th century Chotanagpur and Santal Parganas. Proceedings of the Indian History Congress*, vol. 73, Indian History Congress, 2012, pp. 747-55.

16. Mohapatra, P.P. "Class Conflict and Agrarian Regimes in Chota Nagpur, 1860-1950", *The Indian Economic and Social History Review*, vol. 28:1, 1991, p.36.

17. Padhy, S.C. "Indian National Movement and Individual Civil Disobedience Movement: A study in Orissa

Context", *Proceedings of the Indian History Congress*, vol. 65 (2004), pp. 746-760.

18. Pandey, Hari Shankar. "Early Political History of Chotanagpur in Historical Perspective", *Proceedings of the Indian History Congress*, Vol. 61, 2000, pp.169-173.

19. Rana, L.N. "Introduction of Provincial Autonomy (1937-39) and the Jharkhand region of Bihar." *Proceedings of the Indian History Congress*, vol. 58, 1997, pp.519-29.

20. Rana, L.N. "Politics in Jharkhand during the Civil Disobedience Movement (1930-1934)", *Proceedings of the Indian History Congress*, vol. 66 (2005-2006), pp. 1101-1118.

21. Rana, L.N. "The Adivasi Mahasabha (1938-1949): Launching Pad of the Jharkhand Movement", *Proceedings of the Indian History Congress*, vol. 53 (1992), pp.397-405.

22. Sarkar, Sumit. "Primitive Rebellion and Modern Nationalism: A Note on Forest Satyagraha in the Non-Cooperation and Civil Disobedience Movements", *Proceedings of the Indian History Congress*, vol. 38 (1977), pp. 511-523.

23. Sharma, A.P. "Colonial Dimensions of Regionalism: A Case Study of Jharkhand Movement", *Proceedings of the Indian History Congress*, vol. 53 (1992), pp. 351-366.

24. Shukla, P.K. "Tribal Resistance in Chotanagpur: A Case Study of the Dubia Gossain Movement (1870-80)." *Proceedings of the Indian History Congress*, vol. 62, 2001, pp. 613-20.

25. Singh, K.S. "The Mahatma and the Adivasis", *Gandhi and the Social Sciences*, 1970, pp.125-126.

26. Singh, K.S. "Presidential Address to the Proceedings of the Indian History Congress", Section III, 1977, Bhubaneshwar, p. 382.

27. Sinha, S.P. "The First Birsaite Uprising 1895", *Journal of Bihar Research Society*, vol. XLV, Part I-IV, December 1959, p.402.

28. Verma, D.N. "Some Unknown Paharia Freedom Fighters of Santal Parganas Division in Jharkhand state", Proceedings of the Indian History Congress, vol.61 (2000-01), pp. 733-738.

29. Vidyarthi, L.P. "Cultural changes in tribes of Modern India", *Journal of Social Research*, vol. 11 (1), 1968, pp. 1-36.

30. Xalxo, Abha. "The Great Santhal Insurrection (Hul) of 1855-56", *Proceedings of the Indian History Congress*, vol. 69, 2008, pp. 732-55.

NEWSPAPERS

1. *Adivasi Sakam*, Ranchi, Weekly (English, Hindi and Mundari)

2. *The Bihar Herald*, Patna, Daily (English)

3. *The Englishman*(English)

4. *The Indian Nation*, Patna, Daily (English)

5. *The Searchlight*, Patna, Daily (English)

6. *The Sentinel*, Ranchi, Weekly (English)

Thesis/ Dissertations

Jha, Seema Rajiv (2017). *The history of the Jharkhand movement 1912-2000: Socio-Cultural and political implications* (Doctoral thesis, University of Mumbai).